The Institute of Chartered Financial Analysts
Continuing Education Series

Real Estate Investing

New York
April 19, 1985

Edited by
Tom S. Sale III, CFA

Peter C. Aldrich
Darwin M. Bayston, CFA
Robert G. Chambers
Blake Eagle
Charles D. Ellis, CFA

David P. Feldman
John S. Lillard
Meyer Melnikoff
Joseph W. O'Connor
Stephen E. Roulac
Paul Sack

Sponsored by
The Institute of Chartered
Financial Analysts

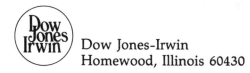
Dow Jones-Irwin
Homewood, Illinois 60430

Additional copies of this book may be ordered from

Dow Jones-Irwin
1820 Ridge Road
Homewood, IL 60430
(312) 798-6000

This publication is designed to provide accurate and
authoritative information in regard to the subject matter
covered. It is sold with the understanding that the
publisher is not engaged in rendering legal, accounting, or
other professional service. If legal advice or other expert
assistance is required, the services of a competent
professional person should be sought.

*From a Declaration of Principles jointly adopted by a Committee
of the American Bar Association and a Committee of Publishers.*

ISBN 0-87094-759-1

Library of Congress Catalog Card No. 85–72857

Printed in the United States of America

1 2 3 4 5 6 7 8 9 0 K 3 2 1 0 9 8 7 6

Table of Contents

Foreword

Cathryn E. Kittell
Assistant Vice President, Education and Research

The underlying importance of real estate as an asset class in investment portfolios continues to grow despite the somewhat erratic course of its acceptability. Its unique risk/return characteristics, stability in fluctuating inflation, and strong contributions to return while providing important diversification benefits make this subject timely and important for all portfolio managers, including those managing tax-exempt funds.

This market is not without its dangers and pitfalls and is not for the inexperienced or uninformed. The presentations included here are all by real estate experts with many years of experience in virtually all forms of real estate markets, through good economic conditions and bad. Their insights and experiences should prove invaluable, not only to those contemplating diversifying into real estate, but those already in this unique and multifaceted market.

This publication is the proceedings from the Institute of Chartered Financial Analysts' Continuing Education seminar "Real Estate Investing," held April 19, 1985 in New York. The moderators,

Charles D. Ellis, CFA, Partner, Greenwich Associates and Darwin M. Bayston, CFA, Vice President—Education and Research, ICFA, were responsible for organizing and conducting the day's events.

The Institute extends its appreciation to the seminar speakers: Peter Aldrich, Principal, Aldrich, Eastman & Waltch, Inc.; Robert G. Chambers, First National Bank of Atlanta; Blake Eagle, Senior Vice President, Frank Russell Company; David P. Feldman, Corporate Vice President, American Telegraph and Telephone Company; John S. Lillard, President, JMB Institutional Realty Corporation; Meyer Melnikoff, Actuary, Goldman, Sachs & Co.; Joseph W. O'Connor, Principal, Copley Real Estate Advisors; Stephen E. Roulac, President, Stephen E. Roulac & Company; Paul Sack, Principal, The RREEF Corporation.

Special thanks is also extended to the editor of this publication, Tom S. Sale III, CFA, for his valuable contribution.

Biographies of Speakers

Peter C. Aldrich is Principal and a founder of Aldrich, Eastman & Waltch, Inc. and is responsible for creating and implementing real estate strategies for tax-exempt clients. Previously, Mr. Aldrich was a real estate developer, a mortgage broker and banker, a property syndicator, and an advisor to public funds, banks, and corporations. As the founder and President of The Boston Company's real estate investment subsidiary, he pioneered direct investment strategies for trusteed funds. Mr. Aldrich was the founder and first Chairman of the Pension Real Estate Association. He has been a frequent lecturer and faculty member at Harvard Business School and Yale University Graduate School of Organizational Management. Mr. Aldrich is a Director of Monarch Capital Corporation and an Overseer of Simon's Rock. He holds a B.A. and M.B.A. from Harvard University.

Darwin M. Bayston, CFA, is Vice President of Continuing Education at The Institute of Chartered Financial Analysts. Previously, he was Assistant Vice President at IAA Trust Company. He is coauthor of *Investment Basics and Beyond,* a managing editor of *The CFA Digest,* a lecturer at the McIntire School of Commerce at The University of Virginia, and a member of the Board of Directors of the Institute for Quantitative Research in Finance. Mr. Bayston has a B.S. and M.S. from Illinois State University.

Robert G. Chambers is Manager of the Timberland Division of The First National Bank of Atlanta. Previously, he was Louisiana Regional Manager for Masonite Corporation with responsibilities for the acquisition of land and timber as well as sawmill management. Mr. Chambers holds a B.S. in forestry from the University of Arkansas.

Jeffrey J. Diermeier, CFA, is Managing Director and Division Head of the Asset Allocation Division of First Chicago Investment Advisors. He is also product and investment manager of the Multi-Asset Portfolio Fund and key developer of the Multiple Markets Index. Mr. Diermeier has written numerous articles for investment publications and is a frequent speaker on various investment topics. He is a member of the ICFA Candidate Curriculum Committee. Mr. Diermeier received B.B.A. and M.B.A. degrees from the University of Wisconsin.

Blake Eagle is Senior Vice President and Director of Real Estate for Frank Russell Company. Mr. Eagle's research responsibilities encompass the study of real estate investment management in the United States and Canada. He recently supervised the research and publication of the FRC Property Index. Previously, Mr. Eagle was a Principal with Monroe Development Company and its affiliates, engaged in development, construction, and management of investment properties. Mr. Eagle is a member of the Urban Land Institute, the National Council of Real Estate Investment Fiduciaries, and the Advisory Council of the Federal National Mortgage Association. Mr. Eagle holds a B.A. from the University of Washington.

Charles D. Ellis, CFA, is a Partner of Greenwich Associates. He was formerly Vice President of Donaldson, Lufkin and Jenrette. Mr. Ellis is the author of several books and articles, including the landmark article, "The Loser's Game." He is a member of the Institute of Chartered Financial Analysts Continuing Education Committee, a past President of the Institute of Chartered Financial Analysts, and an Associate Editor of the Financial Analysts Journal. He has twice taught the second year course on investment management at Harvard and has been a teacher in the FAF Princeton summer workshop for six years. Mr. Ellis received his B.A. from Yale University, M.B.A. from Harvard University, and Ph.D. from New York University.

David P. Feldman is Corporate Vice President—Investment Management of American Telephone and Telegraph Company, responsible for the investment management of AT&T pension funds and savings plans. Mr. Feldman began his career with the Bell System and has served as Director of Banking Relations and Assistant Treasurer. Mr. Feldman earned his B.S. from Purdue University and M.B.A. from Illinois Institute of Technology.

J. Kurt Freundlich is Managing Director and Division Head of the Real Estate Division of First Chicago Investment Advisors. Mr. Freundlich formulates strategy for all real estate investments at FCIA and is responsible for the management of a widely diversified portfolio of income properties. Prior to assuming his current responsibilities, Mr. Freundlich headed the Administrative and Property Management Unit and then the Acquisition Unit of the Real Estate Division. He holds B.S. and M.B.A. degrees from Northern Illinois University.

John S. Lillard is President of the institutional advisory subsidiary of JMB Realty, which serves as the manager of the JMB Group Trusts (closed-end, serially offered commingled equity funds for retirement trusts and governmental retirement plans). The firm also serves as manager of the Endowment and Foundation Realty series of funds. Previously, Mr. Lillard was a General Partner with Scudder, Stevens & Clark, where he was in charge of offices in the Midwest. Mr. Lillard is a Director of the Mathers Fund, Gateway Option Income Fund, Stryker Corporation, and Cintas Corporation and he is also Chairman of the Board of Gateway Investment Advisors. Mr. Lillard holds a B.A. from the University of Virginia and an M.B.A. from Xavier University.

Meyer Melnikoff, FSA, joined Goldman, Sachs & Co. as Actuary following 42 years of service with The Prudential Insurance Company of America, retiring as Senior Vice President and Actuary, in charge of the Group Pension Department. Mr. Melnikoff was responsible for the creation of PRISA—Prudential's Property Investment Separate Account, the first such investment account in the world. Mr. Melnikoff is a member of the Pension Research Council at the Wharton School of the University of Pennsylvania, the Ac-

tuarial Advisory Committee of the Comptroller of the State of New York, and the Technical Advisory Board to the California Legislature's Joint Committee on Public Pension Fund Investments. Mr. Melnikoff holds a B.A. and an M.A. in mathematics from Montclair State College.

Joseph W. O'Connor is President and Chief Executive Officer of Copley Real Estate Advisors. Previously, he was Vice President of New England Life, responsible for all aspects of the management and control of the equity real estate portfolio. Copley is an indirect subsidiary of New England Life and was formed to provide real estate advisory and portfolio management services to corporations and pension plans seeking to invest in equity real estate. Copley's investment strategy emphasizes developmental joint-venturing. Copley now manages real estate assets with a market value of over $3.0 billion. Mr. O'Connor received a B.A. from Holy Cross and an M.B.A. from Harvard Business School.

Stephen E. Roulac is President of Stephen E. Roulac & Company, a real estate advisory and information services firm headquartered in San Francisco. Mr. Roulac has taught at the Stanford Graduate School of Business, Hastings College of the Law, and the University of California, Berkeley, College of Environment Design, and the UCLA Graduate School of Management. Mr. Roulac authored the book, *Modern Real Estate Investment,* as well as numerous articles and other books. He holds a Ph.D. from Stanford University, J.D. from the University of California, M.B.A. from Harvard Business School, and B.A. from Pomona College.

Paul Sack is Principal and one of the founders of The RREEF Funds. With over $2.7 billion subscribed or under management, RREEF manages a series of closed-end real estate equity funds for institutions. Previously, Mr. Sack was Principal of 13 partnerships known as The Paul Sack Properties organized for the acquisition, development, ownership, and management of specific projects. Mr. Sack received a B.A. in economics from Harvard College, an M.B.A. from Harvard Business School, and a Ph.D. in political economy from the University of California at Berkeley.

Tom S. Sale III, CFA, is Professor and Head of the Department of Economics and Finance at

Louisiana Tech University where he teaches investments and serves on the advisory committee to the Center for Real Estate Studies. Mr. Sale is the current President of the Southwestern Finance Association and is a member of the Institute of Chartered Financial Analysts' Council of Examiners. He received his B.A. from Tulane University, M.A. from Duke University, and Ph.D. from Louisiana State University.

Gary G. Schlarbaum, CFA, is a Vice President of the Asset Allocation Division of First Chicago Investment Advisors. Previously, Mr. Schlarbaum was Professor of Finance at the Krannert Graduate School of Management of Purdue University. He has a long list of publications in leading academic and professional journals and has spoken to numerous professional financial associations. Mr. Schlarbaum is Chairman of the Portfolio Management Sub-Committee of the ICFA Candidate Curriculum Committee. He has a B.A. in economics and mathematics from Coe College and a Ph.D. in applied economics from the University of Pennsylvania.

Overview of the Seminar

Tom S. Sale III, Ph.D., CFA
Editor

Real estate has received much attention in recent years as a possible complement to traditional financial assets in individual and institutional portfolios. The real estate field is complex and varied, and investing in it demands considerable expertise and specialized knowledge. Potential real estate investments range from office buildings and industrial warehouses to shopping centers and southern pine timberlands, with each requiring unique analytical insights. Financing and property management arrangements present an almost bewildering array of alternatives.

CONCERNS ABOUT REAL ESTATE INVESTING

Real estate ownership has not been attractive to many potential institutional investors for several reasons. First, real estate has been perceived as a complicated, high-risk investment area where little standardization exists. Second, the management commitment required to produce the highest returns from each property has discouraged institutional investors, especially those who prefer the role of passive investors. Third, the unique requirements of real estate appraisal and analysis has deterred many portfolio managers from recommending real estate investments. Additionally, real estate markets have been characterized by inadequate data concerning the historical returns and risk of the various types of possible investments. Portfolio managers have sought return data from different geographic areas, across property types, and over varying economic conditions and time periods. The paucity of return data, the absence of risk measures, and the inability to correlate real estate returns with stock and bond returns has been a continuing problem.

Finally, nontaxable investors have been largely unable to capture the potential tax benefits of real estate investing. Since real estate prices frequently reflect the capitalized tax benefits that would accrue to taxable investors, real estate properties frequently have appeared overpriced to nontaxable investors. For these and other reasons, institutional investors have traditionally been reluctant to allocate significant portions of their portfolio assets to real estate investments.

ATTRACTIONS OF REAL ESTATE INVESTMENTS

Institutional investors today are considering a much wider range of investment vehicles than they did several years ago. The widened search for investment vehicles can be attributed, in part, to ERISA and its much-enlarged definitions of prudence and diversification. Also, the need to know more about this asset and its attributes has generated increasing awareness of its potential usefulness as a portfolio asset. In turn, this has caused the industry to begin to provide the data and details required by investors for informed decision making.

More specifically, this increased interest arises from three main observations. First, real estate constitutes the largest share of American wealth. Recognizing that a perfectly diversified portfolio is composed of assets in proportion to their prevalence in the marketplace, plan sponsors and portfolio managers interested in diversified portfolios will want to allocate substantial portions of their portfolios to real estate assets. There is increasing evidence that the addition of property to a multiasset portfolio provides fundamental diversification, reducing the *volatility* of total returns without reducing the *level* of returns. Second, real estate is considered to provide an excellent hedge against inflation. Finally, real estate assets offer attractive total returns. In addition to the current income stream from rentals, the prospects for growth in both rental income and property value are attractive when compared to expected returns from financial assets.

Once the decision is made to commit funds to real estate, portfolio managers must recognize that they are dealing with an asset type that differs substantially from the more familiar financial assets. Real estate investments possess several unique characteristics. No two properties are perfectly alike, even though they may be substitutes for each other. Values depend importantly upon how adjacent properties are used and on local and regional economic conditions. Properties require active management of a specialized nature to produce the highest returns. Additionally, real estate markets tend to be less efficient than the markets for securities. Real estate ordinarily is not traded in national markets and transactions are infrequent. This relative inefficiency may produce some limitations, but it also provides the potential for greater-than-normal returns for those willing to do the necessary research.

REVIEW OF THE PRESENTATIONS

Meyer Melnikoff, a pioneer in the area of real estate investments for pension funds, first reviewed the changing interests of pension fund portfolio managers from bonds to stocks and, most recently, to real estate. He asserted that the appropriateness of real estate investments for prudently managed pension funds has now been established. He then addressed the important question of property investment performance, via figures and tables designed to provide portfolio managers with quantitative evidence concerning the risks and rewards of real estate investing. Based upon the data, Meyer concluded that real estate is no more volatile than traditional financial assets and that adding property to a portfolio reduces the volatility of total long-term returns without reducing the level of these returns.

Paul Sack provided a practical and interesting discussion of factors that influence property values. A review of this presentation reveals the specialized nature of investments in such diverse real estate properties as office buildings, industrial warehouses, and shopping centers. Paul's presentation emphasized the importance of obtaining professional property management to achieve the highest returns from a real estate investment.

Peter Aldrich focused upon two important developments in the current real estate market. First, he discussed why the markets for REITs, commercial office buildings, and apartments are in disequilibrium. Peter was concerned with the prevalence of what he considered to be an excessively optimistic view of the growth potential of such assets. Second, he reviewed the new instruments and securities that permit real estate investments to be passive. This process, described

as the securitization of real estate, is viewed as a necessary step in the development of a mature, national real estate capital market.

John Lillard pointed out that in real estate, as in other areas, there are almost always exceptions to widely held rules. John reviewed 10 rules of real estate investing that many portfolio managers live by. However, he clearly illustrated how blind acceptance of these rules, or "myths," can produce disappointing results. John's insights are important to anyone contemplating real estate investments.

Steve Roulac presented a wide range of comments concerning real estate investing. He discussed the strategies necessary for successful real estate investing, a market he sees as a "winners game." These strategies necessarily differ greatly from those employed in the management of corporate securities, which he sees as a "losers game." Steve reviewed the differences between real estate analysis and security analysis, asserting that the processes are significantly different and require different attributes. In contrast to financial markets, real estate is traded in inefficient markets. Trades are infrequent, there is a limited information base, skill levels of market participants vary greatly, and negotiating skill is more important in real estate markets than in financial markets. In his view, real estate markets are more amenable to monopoly of knowledge and buying power than are financial markets. Techniques that work in efficient financial markets will not work as well in inefficient real estate markets. Looking to the future, Steve anticipates that more investors will become real estate market participants. In the meantime, significant rewards await those who are willing to work hard enough to exploit the existing market inefficiencies.

Blake Eagle accepted the challenge of discussing the problems of real estate performance measurement, a discipline that today is at about the same stage of development as the measurement of the stock market was at the beginning of this century. He reviewed the problems inherent in any attempt to measure real estate performance over time, including the uniqueness of each transaction, the problem of appraisals in the absence of a sale, and the difficulties in obtaining accurate and consistent price information. Blake detailed the importance of reliable real estate performance data and the development of the flow of data now available. Institutional investors have demanded such information and, as their real estate holdings have increased, institutions have been the source of the necessary data. Blake concluded by reviewing the construction of the Frank Russell Company's Property Index and discussing the performance of that index and its various components relative to other indexes.

Joe O'Connor took us into the real estate development process, which includes planning and design, feasibility studies, obtaining the needed regulatory approvals, financing, construction, leasing, and the operational phase. He reviewed three critical factors in projecting real estate yields and discussed three investing strategies. Finally, Joe shared the actual return and risk experience involved in developing a large real estate portfolio. He concluded that the risks associated with real estate development have been lower than many would assume, while the returns have been quite attractive.

Robert Chambers introduced an interesting real estate investment alternative—southern pine timberlands. His view was that, in addition to enjoying excellent market prospects, southern pine timberland, when properly managed, may produce sufficient physical growth to enhance a tract's value even if unit timber prices fall. Bob introduced us to pulpwood and sawtimber pricing and suggested that timberland deserves consideration for addition to a diversified portfolio.

David Feldman provided a review of the real estate investment component of AT&T's Investment Fund. He discussed the plan's objectives, the investment vehicles used in developing the real estate portfolio, the factors used in controlling the real estate investing process, and AT&T's criteria for evaluating managers and measuring performance. David's review of the real estate investing experience of a major institutional investor was another extremely valuable seminar element.

As an addendum, this Proceedings includes as an appendix an interesting paper not presented at the seminar but included because it is directly related to the purposes of the program. The authors have kindly permitted its publication here. The paper addresses the question of what weight real estate assets should be given in a diversified portfolio, in a manner that provides intellectual rigor to the portfolio allocation decision. The paper further substantiates the observation that real estate is a legitimate, perhaps very valuable, component in a diversified portfolio. The authors have included an excellent bibliography which will be of interest to anyone seeking additional readings on the subject of real estate investing.

The Attractiveness of Real Estate Investments for Pension Funds

Meyer Melnikoff

This paper focuses on the role of real estate in a pension fund. Although there are, undoubtedly, many distinctions between the analysis appropriate for a taxable and a tax-exempt investor, the conclusions would be similar: Real estate should play a significant role in the investment process for both types of investors.

THE CASE FOR PENSION FUND INVESTMENT IN PROPERTY

The case for pension fund investment in real property, or real estate equities, rests primarily on five interrelated attributes.

- *Desirable diversification*—Property is an asset form with many fundamental characteristics that distinguish it from both stocks and bonds.
- *Resistance to inflation*—In periods of unexpected high inflation, when real returns on stocks and bonds tend, on average, to become negative, property tends to continue to provide a positive real return. The United States is now experiencing a disinflation which is cyclical and exogenously induced, as distinguished from a disinflation which would be secular and based upon a fundamental internal restructuring of our economy. Accordingly, it is prudent to include property investments in large pension plans and to recognize the probability that inflation may accelerate occasionally in the future. Even if the average rate of inflation is sustained at a low level, periodic accelerations are likely to develop.
- *Attractive total return*—Property, as an equity, provides a current income of 7 to 9 percent (after investment management expenses, which tend to be higher than for financial assets); also, prospects for growth in income and in value bring the estimated total annual return to 12 to 14 percent, which compares well with estimated returns from financial assets.

- *Low volatility*—Property, as an asset form, has lower volatility than stocks and bonds.
- *High value-added result*—Adding property to a pension fund produces a high value-added result—a significant reduction in total fund volatility, without reduction in the long-term total fund rate of return.

The appropriateness of real property, or real estate equities, for prudent pension fund investment appears to have been established in the United States in the period since 1970. U.S. private pension funds' growing acceptance of real estate equities is indicated in Table 1, excerpted from the 1983 and 1985 *Reports on Large Corporate Pensions* by Greenwich Associates. According to the reports, at the end of 1984, pension funds of more than 75 percent of the companies with plan assets over $500 million held real estate equities. As shown in Table 2, excerpted from the Greenwich Associates' 1983 and 1985 *Reports on Public Pension Funds*, public pension funds have also been increasing their use of property, but they are not yet at the level of the larger private plans.

HISTORICAL OVERVIEW

A brief history of pension investment in the United States will provide useful perspective. A general pension movement, even on a small scale, did not begin until about 1920, when Congress established the Federal Civil Service Retirement Plan. The enactment of the Social Security Act in 1935 provided a major stimulus to pensions. Substantial expansion took place during World War II.

Until about 1950, most pension funds were invested exclusively in fixed-income investments. Whether held by a trust company, an insurance company, or managed in-house, the funds rarely included any equities. In fact, the institutional resistance to stocks for pension funds was deeply ingrained in that period (and remained so until about 1948). In 1950, only 7

TABLE 1. Percentage of large private pension funds investing in property

Fortune rank	1976	1980	1982	1984
001–100	22%	51%	71%	74%
101–200	13	37	50	56
201–300	11	33	43	42
301–400	7	18	46	46
401–500	4	16	26	25
501–600	2	14	17	NA
601–700	2	14	20	NA
701–800	5	14	14	NA
801–900	9	12	19	NA
901–1000	7	6	15	NA
Total industrials	9	24	36	52
Total utilities	16	22	35	49
Large	NA	25	48	65
Medium	NA	20	27	42
Retail	11	20	44	48
Transportation	8	13	33	37
Diversified services	NA	NA	52	46
Plan assets, millions				
Over $500	35	54	71	76
$251–$500	29	40	59	57
101– 250	10	21	46	50
51– 100	9	17	34	34
31– 50	9	18	28	26
21– 30	6	15	21	22
16– 20	5	16	20	25
11– 15	11	7	16	30
5– 10	5	9	16	16
Under 5	1	5	13	16
Total companies	10	22	36	42

Note: NA—not available.
Source: Greenwich Associates.

TABLE 2. Percentage of public pension funds investing in property

Type of fund	1982	1984
State fund	28%	45%
Municipal fund	16	26
Large	33	56
Medium	13	18
Plan assets, millions		
Over $500	36	54
$250–$500	36	48
100– 250	21	35
50– 100	9	11
25– 50	13	13
Under 25	2	11

Source: Greenwich Associates.

percent of total U.S. private pension assets, which then amounted to $12 billion, was invested in common stocks.

As with many major developments, there is no clear evidence of the causes and events that brought about the change in pension funds' attitudes toward stocks. Undoubtedly, it took some time for memories of common stock performance in 1925 to 1940 to fade. Whatever the specific causes may have been, the results were dramatic. In less than 20 years, the move to common stocks grew so rapidly that by 1968 some pension plans had as much as 85 percent of assets in common stocks. Undoubtedly, a basic reason for including equities was the realization that pension benefits are subject to periodic adjustments.

Whether a plan explicitly does so or not, the objective of most is to provide each individual, upon retirement, a lifetime income related to wages earned during the last few years of employment. Many pension plans also adjust retired employees' pension benefits to offset the effects of inflation after retirement. Accordingly, the liabilities of a pension plan are very sensitive to economic changes, particularly inflation and wage rates. In fact, in valuing pension liabilities, actuaries recognize that there are three layers of increase in wages that affect pension benefits: (1) general inflation-responsive increases, (2) blanket productivity (or improved standard of living) increases, and (3) individualized seniority and merit increases.

If the contributions to a pension plan for a year are to be sufficient to meet the future pension liabilities arising from total employment in that year, the investment results applicable to those contributions must increase their value to equal the increase in liabilities. In broad terms, a pension fund may be considered as an instrument for the collective accumulation of wealth for distribution at a later date in the form of monthly payments to individuals who expect these payments to enable them to maintain their standard of living in retirement. The growth prospects of common stocks clearly make them appropriate for this objective.

The ownership of common stocks by institutions was greatly increased by pension funds' investment in stocks. Pension funds today own a large portion of outstanding stocks and, owing to active trading by some investment managers, represent an even greater portion (about 70 percent) of stock transactions. However, economic developments, both international (as in the oil crisis) and domestic (as in the periodic "economic stabilization programs"), have led to such volatility in the securities markets as to raise doubts whether pension funds should rely on common stocks as the sole means of participating in economic growth. By the late 1960s, some observers of the pension scene began to be concerned whether private pension funds were viable:

Could they offer sufficient security of adequate benefits while keeping the cost of the plans to sponsors at reasonable levels? The possibility of broadening the investment universe for pension plans to include real property was the next consideration (see Table 3).

THE DISTINCT NATURE OF REAL ESTATE

Real estate is a distinct asset form that adds fundamental diversification.

1 Each property is unique in many respects. The most obvious is its location; another would be its physical structure. Each lease and each tenant is unique to each property. This is a fundamental difference from the securities world where each share of a company's stock is exactly the same. Real property ownership is an equity but is different from stocks.

2 Rents on business (office, commercial, and industrial) properties are more difficult for government to regulate than prices and wages because of the uniqueness of each property and each lease. For that reason, whenever the U.S. or British government has considered any form of "incomes" policy in which controls are established on prices and wages, rents on business properties have remained uncontrolled, even when controls were applied to residential rents. To my knowledge, in the English-speaking world, there was only one short-lived attempt to impose control over commercial rents. In 1973, the Conservative Party instituted controls on commercial rents in England. By early 1974, the controls were withdrawn by the Labor Party because of the difficulties involved with administering the law. In general, rent controls are not feasible on commercial properties such as shopping centers where rents are customarily based partly on gross receipts. And consider two leases in a single office building, one of which just rolled over to a new level and the other scheduled to roll over in six months; it would be unfair to freeze rents when the rent is at 1985 levels in one case and at 1975 levels in the other, but property expenses are at 1985 price levels for both. On the other hand, governments can affect property investment through tax pol-

---

TABLE 3. The expanding pension investment universe, select periods, 1925–1982*

Period	Pension investment universe	Effective average annual rate of inflation (percent)
1925–1949	Bonds (and other fixed-income investments such as mortgages)	1.3%
1950–1969	Bonds and stocks	2.4
1970–1982	Bonds, stocks, and property	7.6

* Inflation defined as the change in the Consumer Price Index for all urban consumers, national average, not seasonalized, as published by the U.S. Bureau of Labor Statistics.
Source: Goldman, Sachs & Co.

icy, particularly real estate and income tax treatment, as well as by regulating property development.

3 Although property is an equity, it has characteristics that provide stable income from the rental obligations under lease. Even following a sharp decline in income, a corporation would not normally reduce its space requirements if it believes the decline is temporary. Barring widespread bankruptcy among tenants, income streams for a fully leased property can be projected with a fairly high degree of confidence.

4 The cash flow from a portfolio of business properties tends to change with inflation, even when inflation is at rates that had not been forecast. Although few U.S. rents are automatically linked to inflation, this general tendency results from the opportunity to periodically adjust rents on existing property to reflect the rents obtained on new property, which are in turn based on current prices.

5 Supply and demand considerations have a long time dimension. When it becomes evident that there is a tight office market in a major metropolitan area, it will take several years before the best entrepreneurs can alleviate the situation. Conversely, if many property developers create new office buildings in excess of the demand for office space, there may be completed properties with neither tenants nor buyers for some time.

6 Property is by nature immobile: Scarcity in one city cannot be met by surplus in another. While it is, of course, possible to move jobs, many additional considerations would enter into such a decision.

7 The cash flow to a tax-exempt pension fund from property investments, whether held directly or indirectly through a tax-exempt entity (such as a pooled property fund) is not reduced by income tax; however, a corporation is a taxable entity, and the income taxes it pays cannot be recovered by any stockholders, even tax-exempt pension funds.

8 The rate of current income from property investments (related to current value) has been, and remains, significantly higher than that from common stocks. The discretionary process involved in determining the "payout" to common stock from net earnings is generally inapplicable to property investments, where all net income is generally paid out.

9 Similarly, the nature of a property investment is generally not subject to the degree of change that may occur, either by discretion of its Board of Directors or by government action, in the nature of the enterprise represented by shares of the stock in a company.

10 A property's investment performance can be significantly affected by the investment manager, who can enhance its operations. A financial asset performs the same way, during any period, for everyone who holds it, and no investment manager can affect the performance of the security's issuer.

11 Properties trade on a very private basis, with transactions subject to negotiation and requiring months to complete. Stocks, even in large quantities, can be traded almost instantaneously on very efficient exchanges.

12 There is a major lumpiness, or ebb and flow, in the dollar volume of business property investments available for purchase, owing to their large unit size and the relatively small number of owners. This limits the potential utility of market-timing in property, as investment is significantly affected by opportunity to purchase, and strong property holders may decline to sell under depressed conditions.

13 Property investments, though they provide high cash flows, are relatively illiquid. But pension funds are well suited to own illiquid assets, given the surprise-free nature of their obligations, and should obtain the premium return offered in the marketplace for such assets.

Although they both represent ownership, property and stocks are essentially different and have different cyclical behavior. Adding property to an investment universe provides fundamental diversification.

It is difficult to understand why it has taken so long for property to achieve legitimacy in the United States for prudent fiduciary investors—particularly because property has represented the primary form of wealth for most of the history of the world. And even today, property remains the primary form of wealth in most countries, where many of the financial assets that we take for granted in the United States do not exist and are barely known.

One theory is that real estate investments have followed the changing definition of prudent investing. For years the legal concept was based upon the landmark case, *Harvard* v. *Amory* (1830), in which a "prudent man" investment was defined in terms of how an ordinary man of good judgment would carry out his own personal affairs. Following ERISA (enacted in 1974), the standard of prudence is determined by how a professional investor, entrusted with fiduciary responsibility, would conduct the affairs of a fund. Furthermore, in the Congressional Conference Committee report on ERISA, specific encouragement was provided to include property as a form of diversification, which was stressed as a requirement for prudent pension investment. Another part of the explanation may be that interest in property as a pension investment awaited the development of suitable vehicles, such as pooled funds, to make it a viable form of investment for most pension funds.

PROPERTY INVESTMENT PERFORMANCE

How has property performed as an investment in the United States? Until fiduciary institutions began to take an interest in property as an investment and publish periodic reports and analyses, there was little solid information; the primary property owners were either individual entre-

preneurs who were not interested in publicizing their operations to the world, or corporations that did not provide public information on their property ownership in a way that would permit adequate investment performance analysis. Accordingly, long-term historical performance is not available.

Recent performance of property investment can be observed by measuring the performance of the Prudential Property Investment Separate Account (PRISA). The Prudential Insurance Company of America significantly stimulated U.S. pension funds' move to property investment with the creation of PRISA in July 1970. It now is the world's largest pooled pension property fund and has the longest history of any major property fund in this country. At the end of 1984, PRISA, an open-end, commingled fund, had gross assets exceeding $5 billion, representing about 450 properties located throughout the United States, and held collectively for about 350 pension plans.

Figures 1 and 2 depict PRISA's total performance, including reinvested income, in comparison with other asset forms and the economic indicators relevant to pension liabilities. The PRISA performance shown is after all property expenses and the annual investment management fee, which represented about 1.25 percent of net as-

FIGURE 1

Value of a single $1,000 investment including reinvested income, 7/31/70–12/31/84

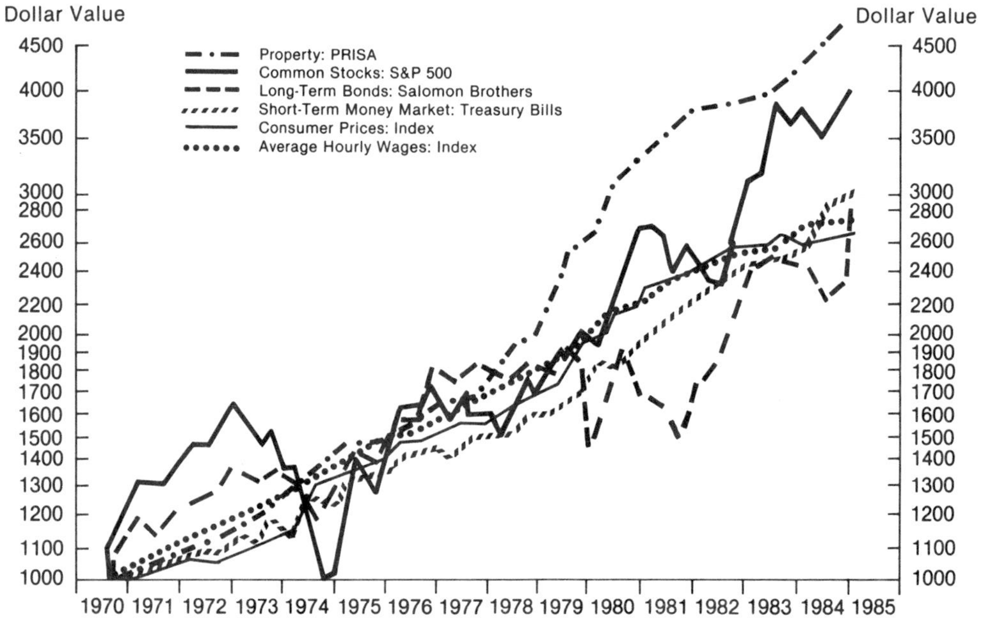

Source: Goldman, Sachs & Co.

FIGURE 2
Effective annual total return on a series of $1,000 investments quarterly, 7/31/70–12/31/82 (real dollars)

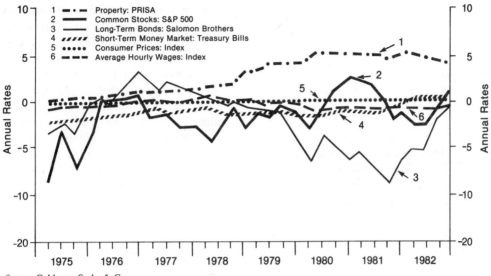

Source: Goldman, Sachs & Co.

TABLE 4. Value of $1,000 investment in selected vehicles, 7/31/70–12/31/84

Assets	Nominal dollars		Real dollars	
	Amount	Annual return	Amount	Annual return
Property—PRISA	$4,837	11.6%	$1,800	4.2%
Common stocks—S&P 500	3,998	10.1	1,488	2.8
Long-term bonds—				
Salomon Bros. Index	2,903	7.7	1,080	0.5
Short-term investments—				
90-day T-bills	2,983	7.9	1,110	0.7
Average Hourly Wage Index	2,689	7.1	1,001	0.0
Consumer Price Index	2,687	7.1	1,000	0.0

Note as to Figure 2: A *series* of payments of $1,000 invested on July 31, 1970 and at the end of each calendar quarter thereafter would have achieved, by December 31, 1982, the *real* annual rates of return shown in Table 5.

sets through 1982, and about 1 percent thereafter. The investment performance of long-term bonds is based on the Salomon Brothers High Grade Corporate Bond Index, while that of common stocks is represented by the S&P 500 Composite Index; neither allows for any expenses or management fees. The Consumer Price Index and the Average Wage Index are each treated as an investment medium producing results according to the index. It should be noted that the S&P 500 closed at 78.05 on July 31, 1970, after bottoming at 69.29 on June 26, 1970. Bond prices bottomed in June 1970.

As shown in Figure 1, $1,000 invested by a pension fund on July 31, 1970 would, by December 31, 1984, have accumulated to the amounts shown in Table 4, with the corresponding effective annual rates of return.[1]

The amounts were translated into real dollars because this demonstrates investment results vis-à-vis the effects of inflation. It is also a very rough way of relating investment performance to the change in the liabilities for already accrued pen-

[1] The relative outperformance of property indicated in Tables 4 and 5 reflects, to some extent, the high unanticipated inflation experienced in several of the years in this period, as well as the unusually low real interest rates in the 1970s.

TABLE 5. Real annual rates of return for series of $1,000 investments quarterly, 7/31/70–12/31/82	
Asset	*Return*
Property	4.5%
Common stocks	0.8
Long-term bonds	(1.2)
Short-term T-bills	0.4
Average Hourly Wage Index	(0.7)
Consumer Price Index	0.0

Source: Goldman, Sachs & Co.

sion service, recognizing changes in wage levels, which generally have closely followed the Consumer Price Index (though actuarial considerations make that comparison more complex).

Merely keeping up with the Average Wage Index may not be enough to match the growth in such pension liabilities, as the index does not reflect the effect of seniority and merit increases on pension liabilities. To achieve asset value growth equal to such accrued pension liability growth, some funds must earn a positive real rate of up to 5 percent a year (or more), depending on (1) pension benefit provisions, (2) actuarial assumptions used to establish funding, and (3) career compensation patterns of the covered employees. It is indeed difficult to achieve such an investment objective consistently over the long term.

The following observations are based upon Table 6, that shows quarterly performance on a real basis, and upon Table 7.

TABLE 6. U.S. quarterly investment returns in real dollars, 6/30/70–12/31/82*

Period	CPI increase	Short-term money-market (T-bills)	Long-term bonds (Salomon Bros. Index)	Common stocks (S&P 500)	Property (PRISA)
1970					
3rd	1.0%	0.5%	7.1%	15.7%	0.7% †
4th	1.4	0.0	7.3	8.9	0.7
1971					
1st	0.6	0.3	3.5	9.0	0.4
2nd	1.4	(0.4)	(4.3)	(1.2)	(0.5)
3rd	0.6	0.7	3.6	(1.2)	0.7
4th	0.7	0.2	4.6	3.8	1.3
1972					
1st	0.7	0.1	0.3	5.0	0.4
2nd	0.8	0.1	0.5	(0.1)	0.6
3rd	1.0	0.1	0.4	2.9	0.7
4th	0.9	0.4	2.5	6.6	0.7
1973					
1st	2.0	(0.6)	(1.8)	(6.7)	(0.5)
2nd	2.0	(0.4)	(2.3)	(7.6)	0.0
3rd	2.3	(0.3)	(0.2)	2.4	1.1
4th	2.2	(0.4)	(2.9)	(11.1)	(0.3)
1974					
1st	3.3	(1.4)	(6.6)	(5.9)	(1.4)
2nd	2.7	(0.6)	(7.6)	(9.9)	(0.3)
3rd	3.3	(1.3)	(6.2)	(27.4)	(0.9)
4th	2.4	(0.6)	6.7	6.8	(0.4)
1975					
1st	1.5	(0.1)	3.2	21.0	0.0
2nd	1.8	(0.4)	1.8	13.3	1.0
3rd	1.9	(0.3)	(5.1)	(12.6)	0.2
4th	1.6	(0.2)	7.5	6.9	0.0
1976					
1st	0.7	0.5	3.5	14.1	1.1
2nd	1.6	0.0	(1.2)	0.9	0.6
3rd	1.5	(0.2)	4.0	0.4	0.8
4th	1.0	0.1	6.5	2.2	1.0

TABLE 6. *(concluded)*

Period	CPI increase	Short-term money-market (T-bills)	Long-term bonds (Salomon Bros. Index)	Common stocks (S&P 500)	Property (PRISA)
1977					
1st	2.2	(1.1)	(4.5)	(9.5)	0.0
2nd	2.0	(0.8)	1.8	1.2	0.9
3rd	1.2	0.1	(0.1)	(4.0)	1.3
4th	1.1	0.4	(1.9)	(1.5)	1.5
1978					
1st	2.0	(0.4)	(1.9)	(6.8)	0.9
2nd	2.9	(1.3)	(3.9)	5.5	1.2
3rd	2.0	(0.3)	1.0	6.5	1.6
4th	1.8	0.3	(3.8)	(6.6)	5.8
1979					
1st	3.1	(0.8)	(1.4)	3.9	1.4
2nd	3.6	(1.3)	0.9	(0.9)	4.3
3rd	3.1	(0.8)	(5.1)	4.3	1.6
4th	2.9	(0.1)	(10.5)	(2.7)	1.8
1980					
1st	4.3	(1.1)	(17.1)	(8.0)	3.5
2nd	3.3	(0.9)	21.1	9.9	1.4
3rd	1.7	0.6	(12.5)	9.4	2.5
4th	2.7	0.7	(1.4)	6.6	0.9
1981					
1st	2.6	0.8	(3.6)	(1.2)	0.7
2nd	2.3	1.2	(4.5)	(4.5)	1.8
3rd	2.9	0.6	(11.9)	(12.8)	1.0
4th	0.8	2.0	12.0	6.1	2.4
1982					
1st	0.6	2.5	3.0	(7.8)	1.3
2nd	2.6	0.3	(0.2)	(3.1)	(1.2)
3rd	0.9	1.3	20.3	10.4	0.0
4th	(0.3)	0.2	11.9	18.6	0.4

* To capture the full effect of the recovery in stocks from the S&P 500's bottom of 69.29 on June 26, 1970, this analysis begins on June 30, 1970, even though PRISA experience begins on July 31, 1970.
† Two months, from July 31, 1970.
Source: Goldman, Sachs & Co.

1 Over the entire 50 quarters, the volatility of performance (which some define as "risk") for each range of quarterly inflation is, in decreasing order, stocks, bonds, property, and short-term investments; in some shorter periods, however, bonds were more volatile than stocks.

2 As the inflation rate increases, the effective average real rate of return of short-term investments, long-term bonds, and stocks generally decreases. For property, the pattern is quite different: The effective average quarterly real return is almost as high for quarters with a CPI increase of 2 percent or more, at 0.8 percent, as for quarters with an increase below 2 percent, at 0.9 percent.

3 For quarters with a CPI increase of 2 percent or more (in the quarter, not annualized), only property has a positive effective average quarterly real return.

Points 2 and 3, which relate to the real asset value sensitivity of the three primary asset forms over this 12.5-year interval, are depicted symbolically in Table 8.

It should be realized that in the 12.5-year period on which Table 8 is based, which is short by historical standards, unanticipated inflation at relatively high rates persisted for several years. There can be no assurance that the same results would be obtained under similar conditions in the future.

TABLE 7. Analysis of U.S. quarterly investment performance in real dollars, 6/30/70–12/31/82

Quarterly increase in CPI	No. of quarters	Average increase in CPI	Short-term money market*				Long-term bonds†			
			Quarterly real return			Quarters with negative real return	Quarterly real return			Quarters with negative real return
			Effective average	High	Low		Effective average	High	Low	
Under 1%	11	0.6%	0.8%	2.5%	0.1%	—	5.8%	20.3%	0.3%	—
1–2%	15	1.4	0.1	0.6	(0.4)	7	0.4	7.5	(12.5)	7
2–3%	17	2.4	(0.2)	1.2	(1.3)	12	(2.9)	6.7	(10.5)	14
3% or more	7	3.4	(1.1)	(0.8)	(1.4)	7	(2.6)	21.1	(17.1)	5
Total/average	50	1.9	0.0	2.5	(1.4)	26	0.0	21.1	(17.1)	26

Quarterly increase in CPI	Common stocks††				Property§§			
	Quarterly real return			Quarters with negative real return	Quarterly real return			Quarters with negative real return
	Effective average	High	Low		Effective average	High	Low	
Under 1%	5.6%	18.6%	(7.8)%	3	0.8%	2.4%	0.0%	—
1–2%	3.4	21.0	(12.6)	5	1.1	5.8	(0.5)	1
2–3%	(3.0)	6.8	(12.8)	11	0.5	1.8	(1.2)	5
3% or more	(4.2)	9.9	(27.4)	4	1.4	4.3	(1.4)	2
Total/average	0.6	21.0	(27.4)	23	0.9	5.8	(1.4)	8

* Treasury bills.
† Salomon Bros. Index.
†† S&P 500.
§§ PRISA from July 31, 1970.
Source: Goldman, Sachs & Co.

The relative performance of stocks and property resembles the fable of the hare and the tortoise. Professor Roger F. Murry, an elder statesman of U.S. investment research and policy in the academic and financial worlds, has observed that the prices of both stocks and property adjust to changes in general price levels; however, stocks adjust on a lagged basis, after inflation subsides, while property adjusts on a coincident basis, as inflation occurs.

Earlier, we referred to the five interrelated attributes of property on which the case for pension fund investment rests: desirable diversification, resistance to inflation, attractive total return, low volatility, and high value-added results. All five attributes can be analyzed statistically, using the experience of PRISA for the 13-year period from 1971 through 1983. An appropriate caution is that this analysis does not recognize the greater illiquidity of property. Table 9 presents an analysis of nominal and real annual rates of return; Table 10 does the same for real quarterly rates.

Figure 3 shows the relationship between real rates of return and inflation for stocks and property. The effective quarterly average rate of return is shown for each asset form at the then current inflation rate. The trend line for common stocks shows the tendency for their real rate of return to decline as inflation rises. For property, the real rate of return is almost invariant relative to inflation, with a slight upward slope at very high rates of inflation.

Table 11 presents an analysis of blended quarterly real rates of return based on the same results. The best performing model, chosen as the one with the largest number in the top line and an attractive number in the bottom line, is

TABLE 8. Real asset value sensitivity to inflation, 6/30/70–12/31/82

	Quarterly rate of inflation		
	Low (under 1 percent)	Moderate (1 percent– 2 percent)	High (2 percent or more)
Bonds	++	+	—
Stock	++	++	—
Property	+	+	+

Source: Goldman, Sachs & Co.

TABLE 9. Statistical analysis of nominal and real annual returns, 1971–1983

	(1)	(2)	(3)	(4)	(5)
		Short-term	Long-term		
		investments	bonds	Common	
	Consumer	(90-day	(Salomon	stocks	Property
	price index	T-bills)	Bros.)	(S&P 500)	(PRISA)
			Nominal Rates		
Effective average	—	7.7%	6.7%	9.3%	11.5%
Mean	7.5%	8.3	7.1	10.8	11.7
Median	7.0	7.7	1.7	18.3	9.2
Maximum	13.3	15.6	43.7	37.3	23.9
Minimum	3.4	4.1	(4.2)	(26.6)	4.3
Range	9.9	11.5	47.9	63.9	19.6
Standard deviation	3.6	3.5	13.1	19.0	6.5
Correlation matrix					
CPI	1.0				
Short-term assets	0.5	1.0			
Long-term bonds	(0.6)	(0.1)	1.0		
Common stocks	(0.3)	0.0	0.4	1.0	
Property	0.8	0.5	(0.6)	0.1	1.0
			Real rates		
Effective average		0.2%	(0.8)%	1.7%	3.8%
Mean		0.3	0.2	3.4	3.8
Median		(0.7)	(4.7)	10.4	3.5
Maximum		6.4	38.4	28.1	9.8
Minimum		(3.9)	15.5	(34.3)	(3.0)
Range		10.3	53.9	62.4	12.7
Standard deviation		3.0	14.8	18.7	3.9
Correlation matrix					
CPI	1.0				
Short-term assets	(0.6)	1.0			
Long-term bonds	(0.8)	0.7	1.0		
Common stocks	(0.5)	0.4	0.5	1.0	
Property	0.3	0.0	(0.4)	0.3	1.0

Source: Goldman, Sachs & Co.

column 4, with an allocation of half to stocks and half to property. Column 4 indicates the effect of adding property to a portfolio invested wholly in stocks; it is particularly striking in comparison to column 3, which indicates the effect of adding bonds to a stock portfolio. The much lower correlation between the performance of property and stocks, 0.1, than between that of bonds and stocks, 0.6, contributed to the higher "value added" effect on overall performance of adding property.

We do not suggest that there are simple mathematical relationships in the real world among these four asset forms. However, we do believe this analysis indicates that property has performance characteristics that make it a desirable and important source of diversification; resis-

tance to inflation, attractive total return, and reduced volatility.

The above analysis of the investment performance of different combinations of assets does not recognize the nature of pension plan liabilities and their potential significance in pension fund investment policy, a subject worthy of thorough consideration.

As is evident in columns 3, 4, and 5 of Table 11, there is relative stability in the property valuation process—even in periods of very high interest rates, such as 1980 to 1981—compared with the volatility in stocks' price-earnings ratios or bonds' price-income ratios. The primary explanation is that property is valued essentially as an "indexed" asset. To the extent that interest rates rise to reflect anticipated inflation, there is a gen-

TABLE 10. Statistical analysis of real quarterly rates, 1971–1983

	(1)	(2)	(3)	(4)	(5)
	Consumer price index	Short-term investments (90-day T-bills)	Long-term bonds (Salomon Bros.)	Common stocks (S&P 500)	Property (PRISA)
Effective average		0.6%	(0.2)%	0.4%	0.9%
Mean		0.6	0.4	0.8	0.9
Median		0.5	(0.2)	0.7	0.9
Maximum		2.5	21.1	21.0	5.8
Minimum		(1.4)	(17.1)	(27.4)	(1.4)
Range		3.9	38.2	48.4	7.2
Standard deviation		0.9	6.9	8.7	1.2
Correlation matrix					
CPI	1.0				
Short-term assets	(0.7)	1.0			
Long-term bonds	(0.5)	0.4	1.0		
Common stocks	(0.4)	0.3	0.6	1.0	
Property	0.1	0.1	(0.1)	0.1	1.0

Source: Goldman, Sachs & Co.

eral expectation that future rental rates will similarly reflect it, and these two expectations will nullify each other. Accordingly, the value multiples change mainly to reflect changes in "real" rather than nominal interest rates. The value of bonds, of course, changes with almost mathematical precision, to reflect changes in nominal interest rates (except for indexed bonds, which, like property, change to reflect changes in real interest rates). The valuation models for stocks are more complex, reflecting changes in the expectations for both interest rates and earnings.

The property net income stream shown in Table 12 can be compared with the comparable stream produced by stocks and bonds, presented in Table 13. Over the 10 year period, the aggre-

FIGURE 3

Common stocks (S&P 500) versus property (PRISA) quarterly real rates of return at various inflation rates, 1971–1983

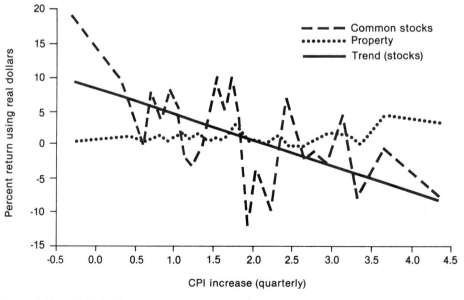

Source: Goldman, Sachs & Co.

TABLE 11. Statistical analysis of blended real quarterly rates, 1971–1983

	(1)	(2)	(3)	(4)	(5)	(6)	(7)
	All stocks	One-half stocks, one-half short-term	One-half stocks, one-half bonds	One-half stocks, one-half property	One-third stocks, one-third short-term, one-third property	One-third stocks, one-third bonds, one-third property	One-fourth stocks, one-fourth short-term, one-fourth bonds, one-fourth property
Effective average	0.41	0.33	0.18	0.77	0.55	0.49	0.40
Mean	0.79	0.43	0.41	0.87	0.60	0.59	0.46
Median	0.65	0.20	0.50	0.90	0.57	0.98	0.57
Maximum	21.00	10.45	15.50	10.50	7.07	10.80	8.28
Minimum	(27.40)	(14.35)	(16.80)	(14.15)	(9.87)	(11.50)	(8.95)
Range	48.40	24.80	32.30	24.65	16.94	22.30	17.23
Standard deviation	8.71	4.52	6.90	4.45	3.08	4.62	3.56
$\frac{\text{Effective avg. return}}{\text{Standard deviation}} \times 100$	4.7	7.3	2.6	17.3	17.9	10.6	11.2

Note: Blended real rates of return used for this analysis are mathematically equivalent to an automatic quarterly rebalancing to the asset allocation indicated in the column heading. Although the relative illiquidity of property makes such a procedure unrealistic in practice, this form of analysis offers a useful insight into the portfolio impact of the performance characteristics of each of the four asset forms.
Source: Goldman, Sachs & Co.

gate property income stream exceeded 250 percent of the common stock income stream and 110 percent of the bond income stream.

It is estimated that U.S. pension plans had investments in property totaling about $38 billion at year end 1984, which represents less than 0.5 percent of the estimated total pension assets ex-

ceeding $1 trillion at that time. Several major U.S. pension plans had 15 percent of their assets in property, and some smaller plans 30 percent or more. In England, about 20 percent of total pension assets are invested in property, with some major plans having as much as 30 percent.

The illiquidity of property must be consid-

TABLE 12. Income stream of real property, 1973–1982

Year	(1) Net income received during year	(2) Value of investment at year end*	(3) Value to income ratio (2) ÷ (1)	(4) "Net cap rate" (1) ÷ (2)	(5) "Gross cap rate"†
1973	$ 69	$1,092	15.8	6.3%	7.5%
1974	85	1,189	14.0	7.1	8.3
1975	83	1,287	15.5	6.5	7.7
1976	96	1,396	14.5	6.9	8.1
1977	109	1,546	14.2	7.0	8.2
1978	139	1,847	13.3	7.5	8.7
1979	163	2,290	14.0	7.1	8.3
1980	192	2,793	14.5	6.9	8.1
1981	218	3,232	14.8	6.7	7.9
1982	229	3,374	14.7	6.8	8.0
Total	$1,383				
Average				6.9	8.1

* Including reinvested income.
† During most of this period, the net income was after deduction of an investment management fee of 1 percent of gross assets or 1.25 percent of net assets. Accordingly, the "gross cap rate," before management fee, shown in column 5 is 1.2 percent greater than the "net cap rate" in column 4.
Note: Columns 3, 4, and 5 reflect the relationship of value to lagged annual income rather than prospective annual income.
Source: Goldman, Sachs & Co.

TABLE 13. Comparative income streams from $1,000 investment on 12/31/72, 1973–1982

Year	Common stocks (S&P 500)		Property (PRISA)		Long-term bonds (Salmon Bros. Index)	
	(1) Income received during year	(2) Value of investment at year end*	(1) Income received during year	(2) Value of investment at year end*	(1) Income received during year	(2) Value of investment at year end*
			Nominal dollars			
1972	—	$1,000	—	$1,000	—	$1,000
1973	$ 29	855	$ 69	1,092	$ 73	1,011
1974	32	632	85	1,189	85	980
1975	34	866	83	1,287	82	1,124
1976	39	1,071	96	1,396	93	1,333
1977	46	994	109	1,546	106	1,356
1978	53	1.058	139	1,847	117	1,355
1979	62	1,250	163	2,290	125	1,298
1980	71	1,643	192	2,793	134	1,264
1981	80	1,564	218	3,232	158	1,252
1982	88	1,882	229	3,374	218	1,799
	$534		$1,383		$1,191	
			Real dollars			
1972	—	$1,000	—	$1,000	—	$1,000
1973	$ 28	786	$ 66	1,004	$ 70	929
1974	28	518	74	974	74	811
1975	27	663	66	985	65	861
1976	29	782	72	1,019	70	973
1977	32	680	76	1,057	74	928
1978	35	664	91	1,159	76	850
1979	40	692	96	1,268	73	719
1980	37	809	99	1,376	69	623
1981	38	707	102	1,463	74	565
1982	39	814	100	1,469	96	784
Total	$333		$ 842		$ 741	

* Including reinvested income.
Source: Goldman, Sachs & Co.

ered in determining its role in a pension fund, as no exchange can provide for rapid purchase or sale of interests in property. However, in a well-designed pension plan, there is rarely a need to make sudden arrangements for unanticipated cash drains from benefit requirements. There should be no surprises, as the plan's primary function is to provide for a series of monthly payments to individuals after they retire, which become more predictable as they approach retirement and are highly predictable when they retire. Accordingly, pension funds are able to accept a high degree of illiquidity. The primary reason for liquidity is to enable changes in investment policy. It must be recognized that real property cannot serve as a source of funds for rapid changes in investment direction. On the other hand, the results shown above indicate that property offers an investment result that compensates for its illiquidity.

CONCLUSION

By combining the attributes of property, desirable diversification, resistance to inflation, attractive total rate of return, and low volatility, property adds significantly to performance because it behaves very differently from common stocks and, therefore, has a high value-added content for pension funds. It is possible to acquire a diversified portfolio of attractive U.S. properties that would, in the aggregate, provide a current income of 7 to 9 percent (after investment management expenses) as well as prospects of future growth that indicate a total long-term return of 12 to 14 percent. Although property is surely not an investment panacea that can thrive unscathed in any economic climate, given the probabilities of higher inflation in the future, pension funds that can accept the inherent illiquidity should now have a meaningful portion (10 to 20 percent) invested in property—that is, real estate equities.

Recognizing Real Estate Value and Managing Real Estate for Maximum Return

Paul Sack

Real estate is not a fungible commodity. Each property is different from every other in its combination of location, design, tenant mix, and lease structure. Moreover, to produce maximum returns, properties must be well managed after acquisition. Managers of financial assets are exposed to much information about the advantages of diversification into real estate and about the pros and cons of various investment structures, but the need to select good real estate and the need to manage it well are frequently overlooked. Unfortunately, it takes an expert to recognize which properties are most readily rentable to future tenants and are therefore the most desirable investments; and not every financial structure and every property manager will cause the building to produce the same return.

CHARACTERISTICS OF HIGH-QUALITY PROPERTIES

The three types of real estate that are included in most institutional portfolios are office buildings, industrial buildings, and shopping centers. I am not going to try to make you experts so that you can go out and pick buildings the way you pick stocks. I will review what the experts look for in each of these types of property so that you will know what sort of expertise is required. In all properties, the quality of the building is in direct proportion to its appeal to future tenants. The ultimate value of the building depends upon your ability to rent it to other tenants when the present tenant moves out—or to make a credible threat that you can get another tenant when the present tenant's lease expires.

Office Buildings

Location is very important. The building should be in an area with other office buildings, generally not in an industrial park or in a purely residential area. This seems to be an elementary point. But observe that there are almost always some office buildings sprinkled into industrial parks; and while they may look very nice, they are almost uniformly less successful than office buildings in real office locations.

Office buildings should be accessible to the residential areas. Because executives and the staff generally live in somewhat different areas, two different transportation networks should be considered, one to the upper-income areas and one to the moderate-income areas. There should be good transportation by public conveyances or by automobile. If by automobile, the building should be convenient to adequate parking. Office buildings should be located close to such amenities as restaurants and convenient shopping.

The inside of an office building should feature an attractive lobby and plenty of elevators. The location of the elevator core is important. If the elevator is at the end of the floor, a corridor will run down the middle of the floor. It will be more difficult to cut that floor up. Floors with the elevators in the center core offer greater flexibility than those with elevators at one end of the floor. The configuration of the building should be such that the floors can be broken up into a great variety of shapes and sizes to suit the greatest number of possible future tenants. The bay depth, the distance from the hall to the window, is important. Small tenants will want shorter bay depths while bigger tenants can handle bigger bay depths. If the distance is too great, for instance, the average size tenant will be left with a long, thin office, with only a short frontage on the windows for executives and too much back space for clerical help. The depth should be designed to fit the market. The width of the windows determines how wide the offices can be inside and also makes a difference in the variety of tenants that can be attracted to the building. An office building should be designed with plenty of air conditioning zones, so that if a floor is cut up for small tenants, one tenant will not be dependent on a thermostat in the neighbor's office suite.

Industrial Warehouses

These buildings can be described as sprinkler-equipped concrete boxes that are rented to store goods as high as modern fork-lift technology will permit. Renters want high ceilings, 22- to 24-foot ceiling heights are usually adequate, though some tenants want to go as high as 28 feet. Older buildings with only 16- and 18-foot ceilings may be satisfactory for smaller tenants in some markets, but low ceilings are certainly something to be careful about.

Location must be convenient to highways and, preferably, to a four-way highway interchange so that trucks need not traverse local streets. Proximity to the airport and to a railway are important in most markets.

Big trucks require adequate space to turn around and maneuver. In a competitive market, tenants will avoid buildings that require truckers to maneuver in the streets and prove difficult for big trucks to enter and exit.

A warehouse laid out parallel to the street is better than one perpendicular to the street. If the building is parallel to the street, there are usually two entrances to the property, allowing trucks to enter from one driveway and exit by another. If the warehouse is perpendicular to the street, trucks usually enter and exit through the same driveway, requiring drivers to snake their way through the trucks that are in the parking area waiting to get to a loading dock. Additionally, when warehouses are perpendicular to the street, firms renting the back space will be invisible from the street. Consequently, back spaces usually rent more slowly and may not rent as high as a space in a warehouse which is parallel to the street.

The bay depth is also important in a warehouse. If a large warehouse was constructed for just one client, a square building probably would be preferred by the client because such a design would minimize the distance from any point inside to the loading dock. But if the client moved out of the large warehouse, the owner probably could not cut up the square building into more than two sections. Bay depths should be short enough so that the building could be cut up for several tenants. Large warehouses, in the 400,000 to 500,000 square feet range, are attractive only in a long thin building, 200 to 250 feet deep, with several truck doors. This design permits the building to be sliced into 10,000, 20,000, or 50,000 square feet spaces to appeal to a maximum number of tenants, obtain the maximum rent and occupancy.

Shopping Centers

Location must offer good access by automobile. The layout of traffic arteries between the principal residential areas and the shopping center is also very important. If the customer has to turn left across several lanes of busy traffic to get into the center, there must be a traffic light to make the turn possible. Otherwise, the customer will drive to the shopping center located farther from home but with more convenient access.

Purchasing power in the trading area is of almost equal importance with location in determining the success of a shopping center. Careful attention must be paid to both present and potential competition with which purchasing power must be shared.

The parking lot design is also important to the success of a shopping center. Parking should be laid out so that cars do not back into the main aisles as other cars enter or leave a space. Customers should not be required to walk too far from the car to the stores. A customer should be able to read the signs on all the stores from the car in the parking lot. Accordingly, an L-shaped neighborhood shopping center is preferred to a straight-line design.

Tenant mix is another important factor in shopping center success. The anchor stores draw shoppers to the center. A typical anchor for a neighborhood shopping center might be a supermarket; a big department store would be an anchor for a regional shopping center. Obviously, the price lines should match the area's demographics and purchasing power. In a lower income area, a Penney's or Sears might be an appropriate anchor. In a higher income area, a Bloomingdale's or a Saks might be more successful.

The satellite stores in a neighborhood shopping center should have a good variety of items customers might need once or twice a week when they are visiting the supermarket. A broad variety of stores, such as a cleaner, laundromat, hairdresser, liquor store, or hardware store, will bring customers to the center because many of their needs can be met. The satellite stores in a regional center might include a mixture of ready-to-wear, home, shoe, jewelry, and children's stores that feature pricing lines appropriate to the area's income and purchasing power.

The shopping center owner, in many respects, is in business with the tenants. The success of the shopping center depends upon the ability of the tenant to make money by having a business located in the center. The best measure of business in a shopping center is tenants' sales per square foot. The more sales per square foot, the more money the tenant makes and the more rent that can be paid to the owner. Usually, therefore, the first thing to look for in a shopping center is the sales per square foot.

SELECTING REAL ESTATE

Because the distinction between good and mediocre properties may not be immediately obvious, expertise is required in selecting real estate. There are a few questions to ask concerning the people who will be analyzing and inspecting the properties and making the purchase recommendation or decision. You should be confident that they know a good building from a mediocre building and be sure they have the right incentives to buy the best buildings for you. Ask yourself if they are in competition with you for buying buildings? Are they likely to be tempted to take the best properties for their own account? Do they have other clients that they are buying buildings for? How are they going to decide which ones to give to you and which ones to give to the other clients? Are they developers who make their profits in development fees and management fees instead of out of the net income?

The organization for decision making is important. How many of them are going to see a building before you buy it? A group of people in a major bank had trouble a few years ago with their REIT. When asked how they made so many mistakes, one of them responded that the decisions were made by a committee of five people in the bank, none of whom had seen the buildings. The analysis was all being done on the basis of reports from people in the field. The buildings should be viewed, not only by the people on the buying team, but also by a number of senior people who know a mediocre building from a good building.

The most knowledgeable people in the organization should not be overextended. It is impor-

tant to know the number of deals these people are involved with during a year. At RREEF, our decisions are made by a team of 16 acquisitions people, 13 of whom are partners in the firm, and whose experience averages almost 20 years. We are offered about 2,000 properties a year that meet our basic requirements of being the right type of property in the right cities. We actually go out and look at 900 of those. Now I do not mean we leap out of our chairs and get on a plane and rush out to see them, but we try to see these prospects during regular visits to each of our 25 markets. We do leap out of our chairs to see buildings that appear to meet all our location, leasing, and price criteria. We probably make 80 or 90 offers a year, have about 15 to 16 accepted, and 13 or 14 of those are converted into actual acquisitions. It seems that anyone who is approving 25 deals or more, for instance, is only ratifying the analyses of other people. I am not sure what the maximum limit is, but it is unlikely that a team of 6 can find and really analyze more than 10 or 12 acquisitions per year.

Once the real estate is acquired, the management of the property becomes very important. Buildings are not like bonds; you do not put them away and clip the coupons once every six months and then cash in at maturity. Real estate investments are fundamentally different from security investments, where returns are the same for all owners. In real estate, the way a property is managed makes a big difference in the current income and in the building's value when it is sold.

An important objective of property management is to capture the inflation hedge that is available in real estate investments. Obviously, if you have leased to a tenant for 15 or 20 years, you are not going to be able to tap any inflation protection that may be built into the property. With a long-term, fixed payment lease, the tenant has the inflation protection because the owner cannot raise the rent in the interim. Thus, for inflation protection you want short-term leases—five year leases are probably ideal in today's markets.

Another important property management objective is to maximize a property's current income by keeping the building fully occupied at the highest possible rent and with the lowest expenses. Obviously, the highest net income will give you the best value when you sell the building. To compete with new buildings in the rental market, your building should be in excellent shape. This is especially important in today's highly competitive office markets. Accordingly, capital improvements and anything that makes your building look more attractive add to its rentability and value. Improvements that contribute to tenant appeal increase occupancy and rent. In shopping centers, the work of physically improving the center is never finished. The property manager is either expanding one of the anchors or adding a new anchor, adding new satellites, or improving the center's appearance. In the regional centers, monthly promotional events, car shows, art shows, and celebrity appearances are used to draw people to the center and to help the tenants sell more.

The need for professional property management is increasingly recognized by institutional owners of real estate. Property management is becoming a highly paid profession in which good practitioners are relatively scarce. In selecting property managers, look for managers who are not overworked. If a manager is supervising too many (for instance, 12) properties, only the most routine tasks can be completed. The long-term planning and capital programs that are necessary to maximize you property's value are better accomplished by a manager with fewer properties to supervise.

The financial structure of the acquisition can also affect performance. The hybrid debt-equity structures which are presumed to be "tax-efficient" frequently result in very high break-even occupancy. It can require 90 percent or more occupancy for the owner to make the mortgage payments. When cash is needed to make the next mortgage payment, the owner is in a poor position to be selective about tenants, to resist the demand for 15-year leases, or to invest in the capital improvements necessary to enhance the property's competitive position and maximize value.

CONCLUSION

Be sure your real estate managers have the experience and decision-making structure necessary to differentiate between good and mediocre properties. If you buy mediocre real estate, especially if you pay top-quality prices, you will achieve mediocre results. And even if you do not overpay, mediocre properties provide greater risk of obsolescence and lesser opportunity to receive the incremental value that real estate should yield seven years down the road. What people who have been in the real estate business for a long time have learned is that if you buy good real estate and take good care of it, it will take very good care of you.

Melnikoff/Sack Question and Answer Session

QUESTION: Paul, please comment on how the current deflation-disinflationary outlook may impact real performance of real estate assets.

SACK: The real rate of return does not change with the rate of inflation. It stays uniform.

As I indicated, we did some statistical work on that. We took a typical building we might buy assuming 8 percent inflation. We set the price and made projections based on that. We considered three different non-inflationary scenarios to see their effect. We looked at moderate inflation (4 to 6 percent, averaging 5) with first stagnation and then with good economic growth. The third scenario projected 0 to 3 percent inflation, averaging 2 percent, and assumed that market rents in real estate would not rise at all. Local conditions of supply and demand would dominate. Projections made on the basis of those scenarios revealed a 6 percent real discounted return in the case with no inflation; a 5.3 percent real discounted return with moderate inflation and good growth; and a 4.2 percent real discounted rate of return with stagnation and moderate inflation. John McMahon at Stanford has approached the problem from a macro point of view looking at actual yields on properties over time. He arrived at exactly the same conclusion; real estate does well even in the absence of inflation.

QUESTION: Meyer, how do you respond to the charge that tax exempt investors waste the depreciation and other tax benefits of owning real estate?

MELNIKOFF: There are two schools of thought. Paul has discussed one of them, which is that for a tax exempt investor to try to get the benefit of the depreciation that would otherwise be available may result in giving up more than you get from the standpoint of controlling the property and its management. There is another school of thought that believes you can get some benefit for the tax depreciation and retain adequate control. You have to listen to both points of view and decide which one appeals to you.

QUESTION: Paul, do you want to comment?

SACK: We are already beginning to hear about real estate equity investments of this type being classified as "nonperforming assets." Real estate equity was never conceived of as a potential "nonperforming asset," but anything can be achieved through ingenious financial structuring.

QUESTION: Paul, how do you approach property disposition and how do you view appraisals as performance measures for closed-end funds?

SACK: We originated the concept of the closed-end fund because we distrust appraised values. It would have been easy to emulate Meyer's PRISA fund and have an open-end fund where you presumably have liquidity and people could buy in and sell out freely. But as real estate people, we distrusted appraisals; and we didn't want to have a structure where people would be buying in and selling out on the basis of these necessarily inexact appraised values. There is probably a spread of 20 percentage points within which appraisers could disagree on the value of a property even though they have the same information to use and even though they are appraising for the same purpose. In closed-end funds—and many people have copied the structure we spent over a year devising—we give appraisals too, once a year, and our clients book the appreciation just like the people in open-end funds. The difference is that money does not change hands in a closed-end fund on the basis of these appraised values. The typical closed-end fund has a liquidation date. Ours is after ten years; some of them are a little longer than that. Of course, you would sell properties under certain circumstances in the interim.

It is interesting the way you approach liquidations, and we are doing that now on our first fund which is scheduled for liquidation in 1986. It has something to do with my comments early about being careful when you buy and be sure you have knowledgeable people. We decided to do all the capital improvements—roof replacements or anything that any of the properties needed—in 1984, so that when people in 1986 look at the 1985 numbers they would be the cleanest numbers that anyone had ever seen.

We also decided not to put the properties on the market in January of 1986 because in January of 1986 everyone will project the value on the basis of 1986 numbers. But if you wait until the end of April, people will buy on the basis of the projected 1987 numbers. The strategy for liquidations is very interesting.

MELNIKOFF: Paul and I have discussed this subject from coast to coast, from Coronado Beach to Boston and we have found two schools of thought on the subject of open-end and closed-end funds. Paul's discussion of how he's preparing for the beginning of the wind-down of the first closed-end fund is a good indication of why we think an open-end fund is better. We don't wait until the end of the ten years before we start refurbishing the building, we do it all along. Why? Because we're interested in the appraisals as we go along, not merely as something to pass on to the participants, but because we believe in the importance of maintaining the value of the properties throughout. We also believe that having an open-end fund permits you to use the aggregate contributions over a long period of time for the purpose of investment policy and gives you a much more flexible investment policy in an open-end fund. You can invest in larger properties than most closed-end funds are able to. In the last year a number of mega-properties have become available and I feel confident that the trend to the institutionalization of the very large properties will flourish. These properties are really available only to very large funds and we believe the open-end fund is in a much better position. The open-end fund can vary the area in which it invests from one year to another much more readily than a series of closed-end funds because it always has the diversification arising from all years. But I think Paul and I can both agree on one thing: While differences in the structures of the funds can be analyzed, the overriding factor is the quality of the property investor and manager organization.

QUESTION: Isn't the low volatility of returns from real estate a function of the way it's priced—that is, on a private valuation basis? How is it possible for real estate to have a return close to that of stocks with a much lower standard deviation of return?

MELNIKOFF: Believe it or not, modern portfolio theory is just a theory and it doesn't apply to real estate and the developers of it never contemplated any such application. Property is a form of investment that has characteristics very much like an indexed asset and an indexed asset is valued periodically on a different basis. Property is valued by using an interest rate to discount the future income, a basis which recognizes the effect of the changing rent levels in the future. In effect, it is valued using real rates of return and, therefore, is much less volatile.

I got an interesting insight into this many years ago when I was visited by an actuary from New Zealand. We were talking about the way of determining the lump sum settlement from a pension plan, a problem that I had been working on recently. In the United States, the right way to value the lump sum benefit from a pension plan is to use current market rates of interest which change with the capital markets. My friend said, "Well, we have a very different custom in New Zealand. In New Zealand, the appropriate way to provide a pension is to offer to increase the benefits from year to year in accordance with the consumer price index. Therefore, we don't value the lump sum value with market rates of interest, but with a real rate of interest." That is very similar to the way in which a property is valued. You don't use the market rates of interest to value an income stream that's subject to changes with the rate of inflation, which is the fundamental reason why the value of properties—here we're talking about what I mentioned earlier, operating properties, completed, fully leased properties—why the rate at which the income streams are valued doesn't vary directly with the capital markets but is much less volatile.

SACK: I've been in the business since 1958 and it seems to me that capitalization rates on institutional quality real estate have varied between maybe 8 percent and 10 percent over that 26 year period. That's as though the P/E ratios on the S&P 500 have been between 10 and 12.5. You know there's been a lot more volatility in stocks than that. I agree with Meyer that you should not compare the stock market with real estate; it is a different animal.

QUESTION: Paul, can you actually negotiate a purchase using an astute analysis of the true rent versus the face rent?

SACK: You can certainly come up with a price, but you probably can't compete with some of the people who are willing to kid themselves. As more people become concerned about these markets, prices will fall to the level justified by the true rent. We're now looking at the soft markets and saying, "How long is it going to take for the market to get well? One, two, three years," and projecting rents flat, vacancies, and free rent over that period which we discount back. We're not buying a lot of properties at the present time in many markets, but I think it's important to stick by your guns.

QUESTION: Can real estate equity be securitized like mortgage-backed bonds and still retain its performance characteristics versus financial assets?

SACK: I hope not.

MELNIKOFF: The performance characteristics would change when the instrument itself is subject to the activities of the market. There exist in England forms of real estate investment known as property companies, which own large amounts of real estate equities, trade on the London market, and take on some of the volatility characteristics of the stocks on the market. They are affected by changes in the market levels even though the nature of their underlying assets inherently doesn't change.

QUESTION: Paul, is it the financial structure or the price paid for the building that causes the break-even point to be high?

SACK: We did a lot of analysis about the prices paid for the buildings by the syndicators. We kept hearing that the prices were crazy; but it seemed to us that the crazy prices were the retail prices that were resyndicated out rather than the prices the syndicators were paying. We found that we were able to compete with the syndicators using our traditional methods and that we rarely lost a building we wanted to the syndicators. It's possible that they were driving up the prices on the types of buildings which you don't normally buy for institutional clients, for in-stance, hotels. But I think that the syndicators probably don't overpay for the properties.

The syndicators' problem is to put the structure together. They want to get as much leverage as possible and so they typically take whatever income there is on the property and give that to the institutional lender, who gets maybe a 10 to 12 percent return. In order to get the most cash out of the institutional participant, they give, for example, a 10 percent fixed return, using all the cash to do it, in order to get the amount of cash up as high as possible. If they reserved a lot of cash for emergencies, they would not get as much cash out of the institutional participant and they would need to raise more money from the tax-oriented people and the tax oriented people do very badly unless they get at least 65 percent leverage. So that jams the syndication into a very high break-even point.

QUESTION: Meyer, how would you refute the argument that reported real estate returns lack credibility because they are based on appraisal processes for valuation as opposed to the true market index?

MELNIKOFF: I have been asked that question many times. Once when I was appearing before a task force appointed by the Texas legislature to consider whether it should modernize the statutes applicable to the public pension funds, a member of the committee asked, "What portion of that outperformance of property is attributable to the appraisal process?" I had never before broken down the performance between the portion attributable to income and that attributable to the appraisal. Over a 10-year period the income, leaving entirely aside anything subject to appraisal and just recognizing the cash flow, was 2.5 times as great from a property portfolio as it was from common stocks.

To look at that another way, if you look at any property portfolio, you will find that the increase in value is directly related to the increase in the income rate. I was once asked why the rate of income as a function of value seemed to be uniform, but the rate of appreciation as a function of value seemed to be very nonuniform. At first, it wasn't clear to me, but I realized that the fact that the rate of income as a percentage of value remains uniform from fund to fund shows that the appraisers are basing the appraisal values on the income being produced by the properties. The real differences from fund to fund are not based on the income as a percentage of value, but on the rate of appreciation over a 10 year period of the total performance of a property portfolio. Over 70 percent comes from the income and only 30 percent comes from the increase in the value of the property and that's directly proportional to the increase in the rental rates.

SACK: We studied the performance of real estate at various rates of inflation. In the lower inflation scenarios, we found that the current income rose to between 90 and 95 percent, and in one case, 98 percent of the total income from the property. The higher the rate of inflation the higher the capital gain component; the lower the rate of inflation, the higher the rate of the income component.

QUESTION: How would a lower tax rate, for instance 35 percent, affect commercial real estate values?

SACK: It is an interesting and complicated question. Two professors in the Economics Department at the University of California Business School familiar with real estate are working on that question. They have found that if rates of return in the capital markets for various asset classes are set by the required after tax returns of the investors, then a lower tax rate should reduce interest rates by two to three points. It would also reduce the required return of investors to invest in real estate or any other asset class. These kinds of things will cause values of real estate to increase.

A lower tax rate may have a devastating effect on syndicators. For example, studies at the University of California suggest that if the entire new tax law proposal by the Treasury were enacted, a syndicator's return on a project expected to yield a 20 percent internal rate of return after taxes would lose 950 basis points. Most of the loss results from the change in the interest exclusion rules and not from depreciation change. An analysis of REITs showed that if interest rates drop between 2 and 3 percent, REITs will have exactly the same after tax return with the new tax law as it has today, so it will be relatively advantaged. This suggests that tax oriented investors will switch from tax syndications to REITs.

For the quality of properties that institutions are interested in, it does not seem that there is going to be a big effect on the prices. In fact, they may even increase as the required returns drop.

QUESTION: What is your outlook for the near term, say 2 to 3 years and the longer term, 10 years and more, and how long will it take for the stock markets to recover?

SACK: I think that the soft office markets are the greatest threat to real estate, and in a diversified portfolio the offices are probably going to underperform. I hope that the banks and other financial institutions wake up and stop lending money for these new buildings; and I hope that there is good, real growth in the economy so that these spaces are absorbed. In some markets it is going to take two years to absorb, while in others it's probably going to be as long as six or seven. A lot depends on whether we have a good, booming economy or a recession. If we have a recession in 1986, as many people, including myself, fear or expect, it could be very difficult for those markets. So for the next two or three years on office buildings I am very doubious.

On shopping centers and industrial buildings, which are very healthy markets, I think there are a lot of opportunities. The difference between an office building and a shopping center was brought home to us at RREEF last week in the shopping center we're looking at. Instead of giving free rent, people are paying $50,000 key money to get into this center, which is quite a difference. In the long run, although real estate will do well without inflation, its role in the portfolio is as an inflation hedge, and if you look out beyond three years, it's very hard for me to see the economy accommodating to a lower dollar and these $250 billion deficits without some resumption of inflation in an 8 to 12 percent range. That's where real estate really prospers; and, to the extent that you're concerned about that, you would want to have real estate in your portfolio.

MELNIKOFF: I won't try to forecast the recovery in the stock market, but I will say that I believe that the role of real estate for pension funds will continue to increase. Within the next 6 to 10 years I would expect the real estate component aggregate for all but the very smallest plans to be 10 percent of the total portfolio, with some of the larger plans going for 15 percent or even 20 percent.

Evaluating Real Estate as a Securities Investor

Peter Aldrich

The first important point that securities investors should understand about the real estate market is that it is the most diverse and extensive market in the world. Current capitalization of real estate assets could be well over $7.5 trillion. A second important feature is the government's support of the housing market manifested through Ginnie Mae, Freddie Mac, and other governmental agencies resulting in a very liquid investment market. In fact, the great majority of pension fund capital in real estate is in the form of guaranteed debt. These mortgage-backed securities vary between 8 and 12 percent of pension assets.

The current real estate market is characterized by two processes. First, the market for REITs, the syndications of apartments, and commercial rental units are in disequilibrium. These markets exhibit the classic symptoms of the mispricing of a growth stock. They have moved from positive to negative leverage by investors acting upon the belief that rental rates and prices never fall. Deflation is only a historical concept to these investors. Second, there is a proliferation of new instruments and securities that allows an investor to buy a piece of a real estate asset with limited risk. There is a securitization of the equity interest in real estate. Securities range from hybrid mortgage-backed instruments to publicly-marketed equity pools by major investment houses sold to IRAs, Keoughs, and regular investors.

SECURITIZATION

Collateralized mortgage obligations (CMOs) and other forms which turn real estate debt instruments into securities are a fast-growing market. The investment banking community sees tremendous fees there. Holders of large amounts of real estate paper see a form of liquification. However, these are recourse instruments for the most part, where the issuer is guaranteeing the paper in addition to passing on some collateral. They are really a method of enhancing a credit rating. They

are not the typical form of real estate debt, which is nonrecourse.

There are also disguised securities in the market. The one that has been most attractive to pension funds is guaranteed investment contracts (GICs). In my opinion, these are nothing but nonregistered securities sold by life insurance companies with a very expensive mortgage guarantee insurance policy. The spread can be anywhere from 100 to 200 basis points. Insurance companies insure that the GICs guarantee a certain rate to a pension plan. The companies take the money, or 40 percent of it, and invest it in mortgages, trying to match the duration of the mortgages to the investment amount.

The increasing proliferation of commercial paper raises the troublesome question of how much short-term borrowing should be applied to capitalize long-term assets. Still it is a fascinating aspect of the liquification of the working capital requirements of developers. The rebirth of REITs is another development attracting attention. Now, "from the people who brought you arsenic, here comes the answer to the securitization of real estate: REITs". No amount of rationale will get some over a basic emotional resistance to the idea.

The most interesting securitization has been in what most pensions have been doing for the last 10 to 15 years; buying shares of PRISA, RREEF, or any commingled funds. These are securities, interests in pools that hold real property. Let us not isolate PRISA or RREEF, although PRISA is really an index fund. It is our S&P 500, our index fund. It marks itself to the market quarterly. While you cannot look it up in the Wall Street Journal every morning, you certainly can every quarter to find out how you are doing.

There is, however, a potential problem with this reporting process. It can lead to overconfidence. In the 1970s, a great deal of money was passed around based on REIT quarterly earnings-per-share reports. In the mid-1970s real estate became uncomfortably performance oriented.

(An element of this has crept into the market today.) But, there we found a market that crashed to the tune of $22 billion 1974 dollars. The public shareholder's equity was lost.

How did it happen? A tremendous number of new entrants led by investment banks and commercial banks had come into the market over a 10-year period. The commercial banks saw a way around the Fed's reserve requirements for real estate lending, and investment banks saw fees. That precipitated a massive, classic mismatch of assets and liabilities. The construction and development REITs borrowed short, issued commercial paper, utilized bank lines, and then lent long. The contract notes were not long, they were short-term construction loans, but there were no takeout loans, no pre-leasing or anything to guarantee a way out of the property economically. The borrowing rates and the stock prices became tied to quarterly performance which was separate from the performance of the underlying real estate. REITs took fees. They made commitment fees, discount fees, and so forth. The underlying economics of the property began to dwindle, just as the underlying economics of American business began to subside long before the great growth stock market died. Short-term performance orientation became fairly hysterical and ultimately all it took was a combination of a business recession and a negative yield curve where short-term borrowings were very high. No one could support the debt. The capital structure of the property couldn't even be supported if it was leased because the cost of short term debt was too high. Everything came crashing down.

Can that occur today? In one instance no; PRISA and the other pension property pools hold their properties, for the most part, free and clear. And they have a low break even, so no one will lose assets by foreclosure. Neither the pension funds, the insurance companies, nor any major pooled fund vendor are going to lose those assets. However, the quarterly valuation of those assets is based on a near "MPT" model. It is based on the presumption that rents will be stable or will increase, and therefore can be treated as net operating income.

EVIDENCE OF MISPRICING

Real estate has virtually a 100 percent dividend payout policy when held in institutional hands. The earnings for the asset are equivalent to the dividend and the dividend divided by the value is the dividend yield. That is the reciprocal of the price earnings ratio. We now have a P/E priced real estate market. Real estate classically has other means of being priced, the cost to reproduce the asset or comparable trades in the market, but when it gets priced on an investor's expected valuation or total return expectation, the value of underlying land becomes the plug figure. Pooled funds today are too often valued as stock mutual funds with high hopes for the future.

We now have a very exercised market where the price-earnings multiple of office buildings has far exceeded the underlying fundamentals of the office building business. Someone is going to lose. Since 1980, urban and suburban Class A office space is being produced at the rate of close to 275 million square feet per year. In 1981 approximately 360 million square feet of office space was produced. Yet the market can only absorb some 225 million square feet a year. We have been over-producing that market for five years. This does not stop the typical institutional underwriter of real estate equities from forecasting the earnings of an office building, throwing in a three to five percent vacancy, and capitalizing that future income stream. Not only is the investor capitalizing the future income stream, but the investor is presuming that rents will always increase, never anticipating rental deflation. The investor concludes that there will be some rate of inflation, and simply increases rents and expenses with inflation, figuring that to be a fair trade and planning to capitalize the income at some point in time. That is also a classic mispricing of growth stock.

Office buildings are not growth stock at present. Office building rents have been declining in real terms for the past two years. They are entering their third year of real rental decline, yet, they are still being priced as a company whose earnings per share will inexorably grow. What might happen is that positive cash leverage could be restored to the real estate market. If interest rates go down, it is always good for real estate values, provided that equity rates of capitalization remain below long-term mortgage rates. Of course, in real estate's distant past no one thought about inflation. Everything was counted in constant dollars and the owner of the real property behind the first mortgage debt received a positively levered cash flow every year that was greater than the long-term mortgage constant.

For the last 10 years the market has been deeply levered negatively. The unlevered owners' current cash return is between 8 and 10 percent, with retail properties even lower, and that has been in the face of interest rates averaging around 12 percent for the period. The old game of financing out the cost of construction, which any manufacturer hopes to do, can no longer be played. You cannot build the asset, finance out the equity in it, and hold it. You have to sell the asset. Congress added to the disequilibrium with the Economic Recovery Tax Act (ERTA) in 1981, an act that added new tax incentives to real estate investing.

Since 1981, the real estate market has been based on the presumption that rents will grow. Two assumptions that appear to dominate the thinking of most real estate practitioners are: first, that rents will stay stable through this awful period for office buildings and then increase with inflation reliably; and second, that equity rates of capitalization will always be below the prevailing long-term mortgage rate. It is time to question those assumptions. Why are we continuing to build all of this office space when it just looks like the early 1970s? Perhaps it goes back to what happened as the American urban landscape began to change.

A NEW COMPETITIVE ENVIRONMENT

Office buildings of over a million square feet skyrocketed in price from a $2 to $3 million investment to projects involving more than half a billion dollars. A local developer could no longer compete. The major mixed-use development business, the manufacturing business of major office buildings and major regional shopping centers became so complex and challenging that large professional organizations with tremendous capital resources were required for efficient operation. A national oligopoly of major developers, most notably in the high-rise office building market, emerged. While that was going on, the real estate lending and equity markets became national in scope, facilitated by the REITs (one of the great residuals of that boom). An oligopoly of national real estate lenders was also developed. Transactions became so large that you could fit into a single room all the major office building or re-

gional shopping center developers in the country and all the major sources of capital. When inflation started to pick up, it became fashionable to do short-term leases. Build the building on speculation, take it into the market, and let others lease it.

These developers lost discipline. The rule of thumb was, and still is *caveat emptor* (let the buyer beware). It is an adversarial business. Removing the basic adversarial checks and balances by creating an oligopolistic market of providers and users caused an imbalance. That is what happened in Houston and in Denver. Boston, which had one of the lowest vacancy rates in the country, is going to have a lot of empty office space in two years.

Why didn't it happen with regional shopping centers? Regional shopping centers today are in balance; the vacancy rate is very low; tenants will stand in line. The original regional shopping center developers, the 12 famous ones, and the lenders and long-term investors that supported them, had chaperons. The chaperons were the major tenants—the J.C. Penney's, the Sears, the Allieds, the Federateds—who went through their own period of consolidation, as did the little shoe store in the mall, the Kinney's, the Melville's, and others. They kept the developers from overbuilding by refusing to go where the economic analysis could not establish a basic underlying market. So that market preserved its discipline and it is still one of the great playgrounds for long-term investors. It is a great business. It is an inflation indexed investment medium.

What about the industrial market? That, too, is in equilibrium today. The vacancy rates are still less than 5 percent, as is to be expected in the mature stages of a business cycle. As an industry that is running at 96 percent capacity, it is primarily made up of local businesses and entrepreneurs, who do not need much capital. It is a highly competitive business and it has the discipline of a competitive market.

The rapid expansion of office building space throughout the country points to a problem that the securitization of real estate is going to encounter. The price structure of the most favored kind of real estate is going to come under assault. Office buildings are going to face some weak times and they are going to go from an "earnings per share" and "modern portfolio theory" priced asset to a reproduction cost priced asset. Those who go by quarterly evaluations will be disappointed, as will those who hold their managers to short-term performance. Those who have taken the time to educate themselves about the fundamentals of the business and understand their own objectives and then act on those objectives in the market will do quite handsomely.

For example, one of the most active investment programs that we have is based on the anticipation of the securitization of real estate. Meyer Melnikoff described how reliably PRISA has produced a 5 percent real return, or 4.3 percent, depending on the year. (It is a little bit like the Ibbotson and Sinquefeld studies. You have to pick your right starting point.) But it is a very durable, reliable real return. Since the bond market has high real returns today, we reasoned that we could go out and offer to lend real estate owners money—old-fashioned fixed-rate first mortgage money—at 50 or 60 percent loan to value. We figured we could withstand perhaps a 30 percent price drop. As long as we made sure there was plenty of cash flow, break even would not be a problem. But we needed to do the transaction in fixed *real* interest rates, not fixed nominal interest rates. Trusteed pension funds are a lot better off as lenders, provided they protect themselves from the erosion of bond value occasioned by high interest rates or indirectly by inflation. You can get the greater of a 12.5 percent minimum interest rate or a 5 percent real return on a long-term mortgage loan—in other words, all of the economic benefits of PRISA with a lot less risk. That is being done in the anticipation of the securitization of real estate. If interest rates go below 7 percent, for instance, I can make all my gain on the 12.5 percent interest by letting investment bankers strip off pieces and sell them as collateralized mortgage obligations, or sell them as pass-throughs. Or if real estate and interest rates take off in response to very high rates of inflation, inflation protection is the 5 percent real return. Even the inflation protection can be stripped and sold.

CONCLUSION

The securitization of real estate makes sense to the extent that it is necessary to open a market, and to allow people to change their objectives—to unbundle their interests in real property. It permits individuals to own less than the entire capital structure of all the real estate assets. They might want to be growth stock investors or bond investors in real estate. Securitization is necessary to the maturity of the real estate capital market that has grown in the last 15 years from a regional market to a national market where people can act out diverse objectives.

For those in the securities business, there is a very scary flip side to that. Our research group in Cambridge has sought to determine if classic mismatches of assets and liabilities are our worry in real estate, then what about pensions? You have liabilities denominated in decades, yet 96 percent of your assets are in marketable liquid securities, which you actively, restlessly trade; that is, invest short—borrow long, which is unsound. It is every bit as reprehensible as the actions of a thrift which borrowed short (demand deposits) and lent long (fixed-rate home mortgages). The fascinating thing that real estate is going to offer is a private market opportunity to securities analysts, investors, and managers in which to match the very long duration pension liabilities with equally long duration assets.

The Myths and Realities of Investing in Real Estate

John S. Lillard

Throughout history man has responded to myths. Myths typically contain enough truth to be believable. The real estate field has its share of these. Several of the following myths, perceptions, or issues are believed to be true by many people who should recognize them as oversimplifications that people make when talking about real estate. The objective here is to provoke discussion and to help develop an understanding of the income property business by describing some of the lore associated with real estate investing.

MYTH #1—BUY LAND

Will Rogers once said, "Buy land, they ain't making no more of it." That is not entirely true. In Holland they have made a lot more land. In Chicago more land has been created by pushing out onto the lake. Real estate has been the source of more wealth than any other means of making money in the United States and in most other parts of the world since the beginning of civilization. However, in the United States much of the land is vacant, underutilized, and may not be needed for generations. Very little of the land in this country is farmed; yet, more food is produced than needed. Even in certain boroughs of New York City much of the land is underutilized and could easily be turned into apartment buildings if an economic need for such housing was demonstrated.

Raw land has a carrying cost and taxes; it costs money when held, and it produces no cash return. To make the highly risky process of land development economically feasible, developers have used a maximum holding period of three years as a rule of thumb. The holding period may be even shorter now with higher interest rates. Pension funds are buying fully constructed, leased, operating properties. These properties produce an immediate cash flow. Buying land may in fact be a hard way to make money, whereas a leased building can be an immediate cash cow with very little risk.

An extension of the "buy land" theory is "own your own home." The idea that no one ever loses money on a house has been very valid over the past 50 years, but it may not be a certainty if an era of relatively low inflation and high financing costs occurs.

Another investment that has become increasingly popular in the last two or three years is regional malls. Fewer regional malls are being built. When a regional mall has a Sears, Penney's, or Bloomingdale's, there is a franchise. The anchor store owners are not going to go five miles up the road and build a competing property to draw shoppers away. However, everything has its price. The better the return from an income property the greater the likelihood there is a developer with a bulldozer ready to build another property. When the return from a property reaches a high enough level, real estate developers are ready to contest zoning, move some earth, and build a competing property. Also, leasing agents will be luring tenants to lower cost outlying quarters.

MYTH #2—REAL ESTATE IS AN ASSET CATEGORY THAT SIMPLY RISES OR FALLS WITH INFLATION

Since financial assets typically have a negative performance during periods of high inflation, the rewarding performance of real estate during such years stands out. Academics have been attracted by this "negative correlation" between real estate and financial assets. Those in the real estate business are more impressed with the full range of possibilities in real estate investing. Real estate is not a single asset category any more than the entire spectrum of financial assets could be considered to be a single asset category. Short-term instruments, long-term fixed rate mortgages or leases, puts and calls, and other options can be structured in real estate. Also, high risks can be taken for potentially high rewards by participating in the development, construction, or lease-up phase in the life cycle of a property.

Most pension fund investors in real estate are acquiring completed income property, fully leased with fixed leases that have Consumer Price Index (CPI) escalators (office and industrial properties) or percentage rents (retail), and expense pass-throughs to the tenant. If the rate of inflation increases, the cash returns should in fact rise not only through an increase in cash flows but also through a higher residual value. If there is no inflation, the returns will be relatively flat for a broad cross-section of property. Increasing returns will come about from buildings acquired at below market rents, but with buoyant residual values because lower inflation will mean lower capitalization rates and correspondingly higher prices or values (not unlike the bond market).

Generalizations must be applied with great care in an inefficient market in which a building might defy all the rules. Most people in the real estate business think that over time, real estate investors have made and lost money more as a result of the prices they paid and the business strategies they pursued rather than through simple reliance on the rate of inflation. Real estate professionals try to add value through the methods they use to buy, manage, and ultimately sell property. Income property is bought for a stream of income that will be valued higher when there is lower inflation and lower interest rates.

MYTH #3—IF REAL ESTATE PROFESSIONALS SAY "BUSINESS IS AWFUL," DO NOT BUY

When the people who are building property, making construction loans, or holding the listing to sell are all saying in unison that business is awful, prospective buyers or property should be looking carefully for a turnaround. Successful bankers and business people have been heard to say that they are scared to death of the real estate market because developers are going broke or because they see a lot of "for sale" signs on houses. Major fortunes were made in New York City by buying in the mid 1970s. This is obviously contrary philosophy, but it is always hard to see it when it's right before one's eyes. Real estate investors are catering to *users* of space. Let the *suppliers'* mistakes provide real estate investors with buying opportunities.

MYTH #4—TAX ADVANTAGED INVESTORS MAKE THE BIG MONEY IN REAL ESTATE. PENSION FUNDS SHOULD STEER CLEAR

Another myth is that tax advantaged individuals make the big money in real estate while the tax exempt investors waste the depreciation and other tax benefits. The record shows that real estate investors in a 50 percent surtax bracket have obtained 90 percent of their return through economic or cash benefits and only 10 percent through tax savings. These figures have been derived from studies of a broad cross-section of limited partnerships available to real estate investors over the past 10 to 15 years.

The tax-exempt investor can buy land and participate in the growing revenues and profits on sales achieved by the owner of the leasehold interest. The owner of the leasehold interest will provide the tax-exempt investor with a higher return to avoid buying the nondepreciable portion of the property (land). The taxpayer will retain the tax benefits (depreciation) from the improvements while simultaneously obtaining favorable mortgage financing on the building (from the tax-exempt investor). In addition, the buyer who needs little or no financing can have a lot of clout in a market which historically has been the domain of the highly leveraged investor who depended on fixed-rate mortgage financing on reasonable terms that are no longer available. Do not overlook the economic power and structuring capability of the cash buyer in the era of the "golden rule," where the one who has the "gold" rules.

MYTH #5—DO NOT JOINT VENTURE IN REAL ESTATE—THE PROS WILL STEAL YOU BLIND

The old saying is that in the beginning the developer has the experience and the investor has the cash, and that later the developer has the cash and the investor has the experience. The careless novice can be taken to the cleaners in any business. Professional joint venturing in real estate is an acceptable means of marrying talent, expertise (that is often localized), capital resources, tax benefits, property management, and other skills in other to achieve goals. Consider the developer building two properties at any point in time, planning to sell one and retaining interest in one.

Which property will be built with the most quality? If the developer is going to own a piece of one building that is not going to be sold for 8 or 10 years, chances are one will do better by choosing that property.

Partners in any business must be selected with great care, and terms must be carefully drawn. However, joint venturing can offer significant benefits to those who are experienced in the structuring of deals to properly match skills and resources for the achievement of complementary goals, which may be higher cash, residual returns, or lower risk.

MYTH #6—"LOCATION, LOCATION, LOCATION" MEANS BUYING ONLY IN THE PATH OF POPULATION GROWTH

Growth typically attracts greater development (i.e., supply) and competition. During a period of rapid inflation, the higher construction cost of newer buildings makes buying in a corridor of growth worthwhile. The higher cost building will charge higher rents. As leases roll over in established buildings, rents may be increased to track the competition. However, if buildings are resold at lower prices as a result of oversupply, the new owner can charge rents that are correspondingly lower and still achieve an attractive economic return.

During recent years, excellent returns have been earned in well-leased office buildings and strategically located regional malls in the slow growth urban and suburban areas around Cleveland, Detroit, Milwaukee, and other cities that are not noted for their growth. As in all markets, both supply and demand must be considered. In real estate it is important to determine the prospective level of rents that might be achievable in relation to the cost per square foot and the operating expenses. It is value, not what is "hot," that is the key, just as in other investment arenas.

MYTH #7—DO NOT TAKE ON ANY LEVERAGE IF BUYING FOR A TAX-EXEMPT INVESTOR

A moderately leveraged, proven property is in fact a niche in the market for some tax-exempt investors. This niche is between the high tax bracket investors, who regard such low leverage as insufficient, and other pension fund buyers who will not assume any mortgage indebtedness for policy or legal reasons. If the rate is below current market rates (as it typically will be today), and as cash flows from the property increase, the leverage should be positive through most of the holding period. In addition, if the mortgage comprises 40 percent of cost and the value of the property is doubled in 10 years (7 percent compounded), this will produce a 167 percent return on the original capital. Add to that the positive impact of the leveraged interim cash flows in this proven property.

In corporate finance terms, it makes sense to consider leverage on income property that is well-leased just as debt is used in the management of any leasing business. Would an investment manager assemble a portfolio consisting solely of stocks of debt-free companies? To achieve a good return with an appropriate level of risk, the key is moderation and care not only in the analysis of the individual property but in the structuring of a multiproperty real estate portfolio.

MYTH #8—SMALL IS BEAUTIFUL WHEN IT COMES TO BUILDINGS AND MANAGERS

A myth originating from the securities business is that small is beautiful when it comes to buildings and managers. Small cap stocks have typically done better than large cap stocks. In real estate, experience has been that in general competitively stronger properties provide the best returns. Consequently, the "unfair competitive advantage" of a dominant site with an office building or regional mall, is sought after. Similarly, in the stock and bond investment management business, boutiques are popular; and it is generally believed that big is bad when it comes to managers. In real estate, a geographic presence will be critical in any key market in which property is to be acquired and managed.

Staff resources also are very important including architects, engineers, leasing specialists, and others. Increasingly, the real estate market is becoming dominated by organizations that are national in scope and that are well staffed. An active and continuing presence is important in the achievement of a deal flow. Recruiting, training, motivating, and retaining professional personnel should be part of a continuous process in this labor intensive property business.

In combination with the characteristics of

presence, experience, and skills, a high degree of entrepreneurship, creativity, and decisiveness is needed. That "loose-tight" organizational structure, which Peters and Waterman described so articulately in their widely read book, *In Search of Excellence*, is sought after in any business.

MYTH #9—REAL ESTATE IS ILLIQUID AND VALUATIONS ARE MEANINGLESS

Income property is relatively illiquid, but an active market has developed over the years for office buildings, shopping centers, apartments, hotels, and industrial properties. A generation ago, in each region of the country, such properties were owned primarily by a few families, by developers, by insurance companies, and by corporate owners. There were no regional malls until the mid 1950s, and office space was minimal in our post-depression, pre-World War II industrial society.

Institutional ownership is far broader today than it was just 10 years ago. A major developer recently announced the need to sell a major mall. Within two weeks, six offers were received in the $80 to $90 million range. Each bidder was willing to close within a few weeks. The difference between the high and low bid was in the range of 15 percent, showing that all the players in the business are using a fairly similar set of valuation techniques. Appraisals are not meaningless, but the assumptions must be carefully analyzed. Business opportunities continue to be highly rewarding in substantial assets in the inefficient real estate market for those investors who have the skills and resources to participate.

MYTH #10—IN REAL ESTATE, UNLIKE BONDS AND STOCKS, THE MARKET CAN BE TIMED

Comparable figures are available to work with—construction levels, vacancy rates, cap rates, price per square foot, historical space absorption figures, and the like. But, just as in the securities markets, the assumptions are critical. How will supply and demand progress in the building being considered? What will energy costs and tax rates be? What new competition will be faced? The commodity is primarily space at a specific location and not subject to much technological change as is another institutionally favored "alternative" investment—venture capital. But on the other hand, there is a set of unknowns.

In essence, investors time through their buying disciplines and will typically buy more property when sellers are highly motivated, provided that the buyers have funds to do so. Sellers are rarely trying to time, but they may be over a barrel or meeting a need—a recognizable feature of the hands-on property market that may not be apparent in the impersonal arena of Wall Street where the buyer and seller rarely meet one another face to face. Many avoid buying when it is hard to buy, as when there are few sellers, or the properties do not meet the criteria. More properties tend to be bought when there are a lot of highly motivated sellers offering attractive prices.

The next one to two years may be a period of heavy buying if there are funds to do so. Overbuilding of office space could lead to a chain reaction not seen since the brief period in the mid-1970s when the REITS had overfinanced real estate. The banks may begin to call in construction loans that are overdue and are not performing. Taxpaying investors may sit on the sidelines because of the uncertainty generated by the flat tax debate. Later, if that legislation passes and fulfills its goal, a transition will have been made from a period in which tax laws have overincentivized the *supply* of space to a reallocation of resources toward faster growth in jobs (i.e., greater *demand* for space). Rents should begin to rise and property now owned will begin to perform better. A little chaos along the way causing temporary discomfort is the price paid for an unusual buying opportunity.

Aldrich/Lillard Question and Answer Session

QUESTION: How would you compare the future rental of office buildings and their impact on future real estate values to the dividends paid on common stocks today and their future values?

ALDRICH: I just do not know enough about common stocks. I do believe that office buildings have been the equivalent of the nifty-fifty. Pensions have some 55 percent of their real estate equity in office buildings. It was as high as 60 percent last year and most of that investment in office buildings is in substantial office buildings owned free and clear. That, to me, is very similar to buying the nifty-fifty more than a decade ago. If net rents shrink, or stop growing, then people will not take a low current dividend yield. They will price it like a utility stock or worse and it will require a higher dividend yield. Utility stocks are a nice comparison for free and clear real estate equity assets: mildly inflation-oriented over the long term. If you want to change real estate equities into growth stocks, you have to lever them. Without such leverage, they do not sustain high rates of growth over the long haul.

QUESTION: Please discuss your firm's arrangement with the State Street Bank. What are the reasons for creating this unique arrangement?

ALDRICH: The State Street Bank is a big trustee, a very innovative master trust. They run a series of real estate commingled funds for which our firm acts as the advisor. We create interesting real estate investments for those funds, which are not ones to cut your teeth on. It is a series of closed commingled funds that are made for pension funds who have some experience with real estate investing and can appreciate the objectives and the techniques used by the fund.

QUESTION: You mentioned that a large part of real estate expansion has been financed by banks. What percentage of the new funds directed to real estate assets comes through commercial banks? Has anyone studied what the savings and loan industry holds relative to commerical banks

and which industry is more at risk? How do the underlying depository insurance companies deal with that issue?

ALDRICH: A fellow from the Fed and I have done a series of studies on this. The implications of the S&L industry were so horrifying that we decided to consolidate S&Ls with commercial banks. If you assume a consolidated banking system, the data show that two years ago 43 cents of every depository dollar was invested in real estate credit. You might think such a high rate is of no concern because the real estate credit primarily consists of home mortgage loans. But, no. The thrifts have been vigorously selling to Freddie Mac, doing everything they can to lighten up their older portfolios of home mortgage loans. They went in with a vengence to the short-term commercial real estate lending market. They have been the largest providers of capital to the office building explosion which still did not satisfy their ardor for fees they could take at the front end of the transactions. When you need a $100 million to build a building, they'll lend you that and lend you another $5 million so you can pay them their fees. That shows good earnings per share because they need net worth with their inadequate capital "ratios" or "base." What happened was that this proved to be such a nice game and was such a good narcotic that they decided it was even easier to do with land. When the developer buys the land, they will lend 100 percent of the cost of the land, another 5 percent to pay bank fees, the real estate taxes—everything for three or four years, whatever it takes the developer who goes off and gets it rezoned. "I know we paid a price that was tantamount to a value presuming rezoning but that is all right, you will get the rezoning. Do not worry about it," reasons the thrift banker, "and after you get the rezoning you will find a market and then we will lend you the cost of the improvements, the infrastructure, too." That is really where the perilous loss is, but you should not panic too much when you look at these empty office buildings because truly they are worth a great deal of money. They will be absorbed over time and the reproduction cost of real estate economics protects the lender. The lender may lose a couple of years of interest, which is the real problem for the commercial banks. They may be out $50 billion holding nonperforming loans for a period of time—that is all right, they can take it. However, the thrift that lends on subdivision property as described above, is financing land speculation in a levered fashion; when land transacts at a price justified economically only by an anticipated change in use, that is speculation in anyone's book. So I am one who believes that Mr. Volker almost saved the thrifts. He almost did it by incredible genius in 1982; he walked on the precipice. But they figured out a way to get themselves into trouble again.

QUESTION: Real estate appraisals specifically ignore the financial structure of a deal, but value the property by standard discounted cash flow techniques. Is there a danger here?

ALDRICH: Yes, I think there is. I have tried to suggest that a retreat to common sense is the best protection in a volatile or uncertain time. This whole infatuation with discounted cash flows does nothing but create an MPT for real estate. The handheld calculator encourages misplaced concreteness. It is incredible the way these young real estate underwriters say, "The internal rate of return on this deal is really great. It is 14.067 percent." And I say, "My golly, if we can hit it 10 years hence within a couple of hundred basis points, then we have done a marvelous job." These discounted cash flows are self-fulfilling prophecies because of the underlying assumptions; rents will increase with inflation and the basic underlying equity rate of capitalization will not change nominally nor with respect to the long-term lending rate. Those are fallacies. Of course, rates will change. They always change.

Polls show the equity rate of capitalization has been very stable in the last 10 years—not 15. But its relationship to the long-term lending rate has gone all over the block, from positive leverage to negative leverage. You would all be well advised to go back to basic underlying real estate economics which says find a good cost estimator, figure out what it costs to reproduce that asset and see how much of that cost is resident in soft cost interest and land because those are the things that change very quickly.

QUESTION: Given your views of the office market and inflation over the next two years, please discuss the real estate hybrid mortgage structures versus 100 percent equity ownership, particularly in view of Mr. Sack's remarks about the high break-even and low property management guides of the hybrid structures.

LILLARD: Everything is relative and you could have a hybrid structure that would have too high a break-even point. What all of us in the business are trying to do is structure portfolios in such a way that we have different levels of risk and the different levels are in the various properties. So in a typical closed-end fund for example, you will have a very strong positive cash flow. You might have one or two properties on which you have taken a more aggressive position than on others, with the objective of earning a higher return. But if risk materializes you will certainly be able to carry them very well.

We think it is important that every property purchased today, be leased through the next several years—in other words, that you are leased through the economic valley. If all of your leases are coming up over the next one to two years and you are in a market that is overbuilt, you'd better have bought at a price that is well below replacement cost or you may very well experience big problems.

Games the Stock Market Didn't Teach You

Stephen E. Roulac

Those with a background in the financial analysis and investment management of corporate securities should embrace the principle that "strategy transference from a loser's game to a winner's game may be a losing proposition." Expressing this another way, players who do not know the rules of a specialized game such as baccarat should not sit down at the table with a bigger stake than they can afford to lose. Many investors new to real estate may be pursuing strategies equivalent to playing baccarat without sufficient appreciation of the nuances and subtleties of the game.

Differences in market efficiency have major implications for investment strategy. In the less efficient market, the payoff for expertise is higher, just as the penalty for incompetence is greater. This theme is eloquently captured by Charles Ellis in his classic article, "The Loser's Game."[1] The theory is that in corporate securities markets investment results are more influenced by miscalculation than by the aggressive actions of those who ultimately prevail. Consequently, the odds lead to underperforming the stock market indexes, especially since transaction costs and management fees are not included in indexes. With the declining individual investor component of share trades, a relatively small group of unmeasured investors remains to be the losers against whom the "measured" managers hope to prevail. The growing recognition of the "loser's game" has stimulated the growth of approaches that seek to mimic the overall market by achieving broad diversification, to replicate market performance, and to drive down both administration and transaction costs.

A strategic approach to investing suggests seeking those investment markets where the investor has the opportunity to achieve a comparative advantage. While the question of the relative efficiency of different securities markets may no longer be a highly controversial and much debated topic, there is no question that certain markets exhibit materially greater degrees of efficiency than do others. In a market that is highly efficient, investment analysis offers less prospect of identifying mispriced securities than one that is characterized by inefficiency. The payoff for superior investment analysis is greatest where the opportunity exists to achieve performance differentiated from the norm.

Investors and their advisors facing more efficient "loser's game" markets logically search for more rewarding games to play, particularly winner's games. A conscientious search for more rewarding market segments brings investors to real estate. In theory, the more inefficient real estate market should exacerbate performance dispersion. Significantly, although real estate potentially is a lower risk investment medium, the dearth of conscientious investment analysis has for many negated this potential benefit. To some degree, however, these truisms of market efficiency and risk have not been recognized, because of the phenomenon of a "rising tide" real estate market. Consequently, some investors with a corporate securities background may have been lulled into a false sense of confidence.

SOURCES OF INEFFICIENCY

The many factors contributing to a comparatively inefficient real estate investing market include transaction infrequency, property uniqueness, information unavailability, limited and unsophisticated investment analysis, unpackaged investments, confrontational pricing negotiations versus impersonal auction markets for corporate securities, extended execution time horizons, and management responsibilities and influence on investment performance.

As a particular property may come to the market only every 5 to 10 years, not much information is readily available nor can an analyst readily obtain an S&P tear sheet on the building, since such information does not exist in the public domain. Much of the information needed for in-

[1] Charles Ellis, "The Loser's Game," *Financial Analysts Journal* 31, No. 4 (July–August 1975), p. 19.

vestment decisions must be custom prepared for the time, place, and circumstances of the particular transaction. As fewer analysts evaluate a given transaction, so also are much fewer aggregate resources devoted to the investment decision process. Transaction infrequency is a major constraint to a cumulative broad "market intelligence" of real estate transaction information concerning price and value.

The investment comparability of different real estate investments is constrained by each property's uniqueness. Factors contributing to a property's uniqueness include size, age, height, floor dimensions and efficiency, design, construction materials, condition, tenant mix, lease structure, transportation access, road visibility, region, submarket within region, neighborhood within submarket, specific street address, as well as finance structure and tax attributes. Through appropriate analytical procedures, each of these differences can be assessed, measured, and compared, and informed decisions made. This process, however, requires a breadth of market exposure, information access, experiential-based judgment, analytic sophistication, and intensity of effort that are beyond what the majority of participants have traditionally employed and are prepared to employ.

Whereas the preponderance of evidence suggests that superior investment analysis applied to real estate decisions offers a relatively higher payoff than does comparable analysis directed to most corporate securities situations, the quantity and quality of investment analysis resources devoted to studying corporate securities vastly overwhelms those applied to real estate investment analysis. Too seldom do investment decision makers recognize the contribution that investment analysis can make to the real estate investment process. Because many organizations involved in originating real estate investment opportunities stress persuasive talents and negotiating abilities over analysis and decision making, third party economic analysis is especially important. In actual practice, such third party economic analysis that is commissioned, all too often amounts to ritualistic compliance with some regulatory requirement.

The budgets for real estate investment analysis seldom bear any realistic relationship to the decision to be made. While the tendency to underestimate the benefits that can be obtained from collecting and evaluating new information

is not unique to real estate,[2] the tendency to undercommit resources to analysis is extremely high in the real estate setting.

The resources devoted to the real estate investment decision process vary extraordinarily. In a study of the acquisition processes employed by 100 real estate investment managers, the most resource-intensive investment management firm committed ten times the resources to the acquisition effort as did the least serious investment management firm.[3] Although the real estate investment analysis process is evolving toward greater diligence and analytic sophistication, a large number of real estate investment decisions are still made on the basis of investigative and analytic efforts that are more implicit, impressionistic, and random in terms of thoroughness, than explicit, analytical, and comprehensive.

The nature of how a particular property is acquired and then ultimately managed further contributes to the prospects of variability in performance. Corporate securities trade in a larger impersonal auction market rather than the rough-and-tumble realm of personal and often confrontational negotiation of real estate deal-making. This adversarial process contributes to the prospect of greater advantage or disadvantage, depending upon the relative negotiating abilities, circumstances, and motivations of the parties involved. As a consequence, the results of the transactions reached through negotiation may bear more parallels to the inherent variability associated with the pricing of a new issue of corporate securities or of a venture capital decision, than the buy-sell interaction for a security that has traded actively in the secondary market.

The execution of real estate transactions differs markedly from those in the corporate securities market. The transaction process is much closer to the purchase/disposition of a complete business than transactions in the corporate securities market. Real estate transactions extend over longer time horizons, are less certain and predictable, are more complex, and more susceptible to major variation in the outcome from original expectation. As a consequence, whereas a mistake made in the corporate securities market can be

[2] Irving L. Janis and Leon Marr, *Decision-Making—A Psychological Analysis of Conflict, Choice, and Commitment* (New York: The Free Press, 1977).

[3] Stephen E. Roulac, *Modern Real Estate Investment* (San Francisco: Property Press, 1976).

readily corrected, implementing a change of heart in real estate is time consuming and expensive. The "round trip" difference between corporate securities and real estate is reflected in terms of months and several hundred basis points.

Further, once an investor acquires a common stock, unless the position is a major one and the investor elects to initiate an active role in that company's business policies and operations management, the performance of that stock for all intents and purposes is largely independent of the identity, aspirations, managerial talents, and objectives of its owners. In sharp contrast, the performances of real properties very much are influenced by the initiative, creativity, energy, merchandising, purchasing, maintenance, and control of the owner and/or owner's agent. While a minority of corporate securities investors may reliably proceed on the basis of common stocks neither knowing nor caring who owns them, buildings' returns are very influenced by their ownership. Corporate securities investors who do not recognize this reality in their real estate investing decisions proceed at great peril.

Whereas investors in corporate securities do so largely on a passive basis, with few decisions required and no expectations of active involvement, real estate investing brings with it many decisions and the requirement for active involvement. Real estate investing operates in a manner equivalent to requiring the corporate securities investor to dismiss the management of every company in which he or she invests, and then to hire the middle management while retaining the essential senior management and board of directors decisions for each of those enterprises. Each real property should be considered a separate business requiring a 24 hour staff, maintenance of the physical plant, a singular marketing program, compliance with government regulations, and financial controls. Just as many real estate decisions are made on the basis of insufficient investigation and analysis, so also are many properties managed on the basis of insufficient planning and control. These realities create opportunities for the serious investor and concurrently are reasons for caution for the corporate securities investor and professional transferring their attentions to the real estate sector.

The nature of the critical decisions that create value vary significantly between the corporate and real estate sectors. The majority of the decisions by a corporation's customer are not that significant in the overall scheme of their customer's business. Most corporations' customers are reasonably informed and are committed to making effective purchasing decisions, and their associated financial commitments to buy products and retain services tend on average to be of a smaller scale, greater frequency, and more familiarity than is the case for real estate decisions. By contrast, in the real estate setting, the expenditures loom larger. The decisions are infrequent and the decision makers are likely to be less knowledgeable and experienced in the decision. The space occupancy lease decision is in some cases in excess of 10 percent of revenues for a period as long as 10, 20, or even more years. The decision maker managing the building, on the other hand, knows all the building's lease terms, is active in the market on an ongoing basis, and has significant accumulated experience and expertise in the negotiation process. This superior information and knowledge contributes to disproportionate power favoring the building owner. Those investors who participate in the real estate business without such property management capabilities do so at a significant disadvantage to their competitors who do possess such knowledge. The active property management involvement that is critical to creating value in the real estate business is a condition not characteristic of corporate securities.

RISK CONUNDRUM RESOLUTION

The implication of the less efficient market is greater variability in investment performance. At the same time, however, many real estate investing proponents assert that real estate investing features lower risk, suggesting more stability and less variability. If real estate does in fact possess lower risk or is moving in that direction, then the associated implication is a concurrent move to less efficiency, or more of a loser's than a winner's game.

This lower risk-inefficient market conundrum is resolved by the insight that real estate's potentially lower risk is not fully achieved in practice. As noted above, the state of the art of investment analysis is relatively primitive. As developed more fully below, the rapid institutionalization of real estate investing has strained—more accurately, outpaced—the capabilities of organizations providing real estate investment management services. The combination of limited knowledge and casual application contribute to market inefficiency.

Nonetheless, it is helpful to consider why the real estate investment decision process is more amenable to a high reliability than the companion process for corporate securities. Real estate investment results can potentially be projected with greater certainty than can the investment prospects of common stocks. As a consequence, real estate investing potentially offers lower risk. Real estate investment results can be forecast with greater certainty because it is possible to forecast the likely operating results of a specific real property with greater accuracy than can be done for a company. The logic underlying this statement is quite straightforward in that a company consists of multiple factors, in addition to real property, which influence the future outcome of business. These many factors, each of which has a certain range of associated variance, compound the forecasting problem. When one must deal with sales tactics, organizational relationships, government regulations, and other forces influencing business results, the predictive process is made more difficult.

Once one has a forecast of probable results from a given investment, the next step is to look at the means by which the market measures value. In the corporate setting, price-earnings multiples reflect the earnings expectations of corporate securities. Similarly, for real estate, price is a function of cash flow expectations, with real estate capitalization rates being the inverse of price-earning multiples (allowing for cash versus accrual accounting adjustments). Experience has shown that the changes in capitalization rates over time are less volatile than swings in price-earnings multiples for companies. The tighter range and lower standard deviation of real estate cash flow multiples versus corporate price-earnings multiples indicate that the real estate investment analysis process is characterized by greater predictability.

Because the results of real estate investment can be predicted with more reliability than can common stock investments and because the forces influencing pricing are less volatile for real estate investments, the overall certainty associated with the anticipated returns from real estate is potentially greater than that associated with common stocks. Further, the securities form poses additional uncertainty as to how the market will perceive the performance of a specific company.

DECISION HIERARCHY

The investment decision trilogy of policy, portfolio, and security analysis, when applied to the real estate sector, has both meaningful parallels to and also significant differences from similar corporate securities decisions. The unpackaged real estate investment is a negotiated transaction, with venture capital considerations more apt than those that govern prepackaged corporate securities. Although many of the available opportunities are packaged, many investors buying these securities packages are most probably insufficiently familiar with what goes into the packaging process. This investor unfamiliarity is contrasted with their knowledge of corporate securities and the improbable successful transference of such knowledge to investment decisions concerning prepackaged real estate securities.

In the update of *Stock Market: Theories and Evidence*,[4] James Lorie reiterated his conclusion that resources are devoted to the functions of policy, portfolio, and security analysis in the opposite priority and proportion to what they ought to be. This misallocation and misappreciation of investing priorities is exaggerated in real estate investing. Because of the nature of the real estate markets, a framework to understand how the business works is absolutely critical. Since so few managers pursue real estate investing with a logical, explicit strategy, investors must exert more initiative to frame their strategies.

The misplaced decision hierarchy is vividly apparent when the present practices of pension real estate investing are considered. Present institutional real estate commitments in the several percent range are trivial relative to achieving the expressed objectives of inflation hedge, greater performance stability, and diversification. Pension investors' portfolio allocation decisions concerning real estate generally appear to be lacking in analytical rigor. Such allocation decisions are mostly arbitrary, especially when the reality that real estate represents more than 50 percent of the aggregate wealth portfolio is considered.

The overly modest pension commitments are not surprising since many making real estate policy decisions reflect a lack of understanding of the basic long term nature of real estate. Substantial rewards can be achieved by having deep

[4] James H. Lorie, Peter Dodd, and May Hamilton Kimpton, *The Stock Market: Theories and Evidence,* 2d ed. (Homewood, Ill.: Richard D. Irwin, 1985).

pockets and staying power, yet many investors combine a trading, rather than a value-enhancement mentality with a very short, rather than long, term orientation. The liquidity issue seems to be misdirected and not really understood. Indeed, opportunities exist for a differentiated investment fund product based on a longer holding period.

The issue of diversification is intriguing, inasmuch as there is a tendency by many to treat real estate as basically a monolithic investment product. In fact, as many nuances and differences are present in the real estate investment product design decision as exist in designing mutual funds or any other type of investment product. Too many who make a decision to "get into real estate" stop there without recognizing the breadth, scope, and extent of the many specific considerations to be addressed. More specialized investment products are emerging to offer wider investor choice than has been available with the plethora of "vanilla-look-alike" funds that have enjoyed dominant market shares.

Too many investment management firms pursue real estate investment strategies that are diametrically opposed to what they do on the corporate securities side. This results in a real estate program that nullifies the reasons for getting into real estate in the first place and ultimately weakens the effectiveness of primary corporate securities strategies. This perverse outcome is particularly evident when a management firm adds a real estate capability or offers a real estate product that is totally incompatible with the technology, theory, and principles it employs in its corporate securities investing.

Many significant portfolio construction and risk control issues have not been sufficiently addressed. As a case in point, insufficient attention is directed to the differences in risk between a single tenant building leased long term and a multi-tenant office building or shopping center. With the proper structure of lease terms, a single building can come very close to replicating certain diversification attributes of multiple asset portfolios.

INSTITUTIONAL PRESSURES STRAIN MANAGEMENT CAPABILITY

While the real estate business has become institutionalized and achieved legitimacy as an accepted investment, the supply of managers and the managerial capabilities fall far short of the demand. The institutionalization of the real estate business has caused a new genre of firms to emerge, which provide real estate asset management services. Fifteen years ago, few organizations had any meaningful responsibilities for overseeing real estate assets on a substantial scale. Yet today, at least 500 organizations provide real estate asset management services. The growth challenge is especially evident in the expected increase in pension real estate commitments, from a figure of approximately $100 billion to a range of $300 billion to $700 billion within the next 10 years. This spurt in growth imposes extraordinary demands on organizations, managers, and their advisors.

The number of persons possessing the requisite experience, training, and knowledge of real estate investing is grossly inadequate to the existing and prospective future demand for real estate investment management services. The results of this managerial crisis have been excessive personnel turnover, organizational disruption, and strategic malaise, if not misdirection. Integrating a business that is entrepreneurial in nature with the larger organizational context of the financial services firm during a period of dramatic economic and technological change requires an effort that should not be underestimated. Those managers and professional advisors who have the ability to address these issues in a responsible manner are at a premium.

The emergence of real estate as an accepted and even favored investment vehicle has raced far ahead of the support services needed for smoothly functioning markets and effective participation. The kind of basic information found in the libraries of securities firms and industrial enterprises has been unavailable in the real estate field. Increasing demands are being placed on managerial resources to cope with real estate decisions. Greater competition in the business will mean that the decision frame will be more exacting than in times past.

One of the intriguing challenges of institutional real estate, where much work remains to be done, is in the realm of manager selection and performance monitoring. To understand this challenge, it is helpful to consider the past environment of the real estate investing business. Simply stated, project planning, financing acumen, financial controls, and marketing expertise historically were not priorities, as strong demand more than offset managerial deficiencies. A number of participants realized significant profits in spite of what they did, although some may have concluded that their intuition was the source of their fortunes rather than favorable market conditions. In such a setting, the market for new management capability was not generally recognized by those perceived to be its beneficiaries.

Today, real estate investment manager selection and performance monitoring can be described as driven as much by cronyism and impressionability as by objectivity and insight. Many administrators and trustees responsible for institutional funds lack the requisite information, knowledge, and experience, so suboptimal decisions are a not unexpected outcome. Unfortunately, certain of the consultants "servicing" the pension real estate sector may be only marginally more qualified. The majority of pension real estate consultants lack sufficient market presence and volume of business activity to support the necessary research of the critical real estate markets or to conduct meaningful analyses of investment performance. Many real estate participants are both narrow in their outlook and insufficiently aware of what is happening in other parts of the real estate business. As a case in point, real estate participants are knowledgeable about only a small percent of the services, space, or capital markets; as they tend to lack awareness of what is happening in other parts of the market and of developments in the broader marketplace that affect the demand for output of real estate markets. Such knowledge is fundamental to achieving superior institutional investment results.

The transformation in the structure of the real estate services markets currently under way is in many respects reminiscent of what occurred in the corporate securities markets during the decade of the 1970s. Extraordinary consolidation and realignment of competitive positions and organizational relationships are occurring. An understanding of these changes is absolutely fundamental to knowing how these decisions influence the prices of properties, the types of programs offered, and the investment results achieved.

Traditionally, reporting in the real estate business lacks consistency, standards, and communication in a form that investors can relate to. In many ways, the financial information available in the real estate investing business has par-allels to what existed in corporate securities prior to the 1930s. Performance measurement poses a dilemma in the manager selection decision. Although significant progress is being made in the appraisal field, some investment managers employ an appraisal process that is driven largely by a self-dealing framework wherein the manager's staff does its own appraisals, an arrangement not dissimilar to a corporation preparing its own financial statements without outside involvement. While change will come over time, appraisal questions continue to be a major impediment to full acceptance of real estate by many institutional investors.

The real estate sector lacks a substantive human capital base, nor is there a meaningful broad commitment to extend this meager knowledge base. Few MBA programs in graduate business schools of consequence offer a real estate curriculum. The real estate field lacks a Procter & Gamble, IBM, or similar companies where people can work for a while, learn the business, and then transfer to the more entrepreneurial offshoots of those particular sectors. The proliferating real estate literature is mostly of the inspirational or "how to" variety. Further, the serious general business and economic journals generally lack a knowledgeable readership, while the real estate journals tend to lack an influential readership. It is notable that, of the 2,000 articles on business topics published by the *Harvard Business Review* during the last 15 years, fewer than 10 addressed the issue of real estate decisions in a managerial context. Yet during this period, real estate triggered the creation of more wealth and economic activity than all but a very few economic sectors.

A further implication of this management challenge as real estate investing becomes more institutionalized is the question of the requisite personal style as contrasted to that required for success in corporate securities investing. Those with a corporate securities background may naturally tend to favor managers who are similar to themselves. But the conceptual/intellectual approach that works in the stock market may not necessarily be successfully transferred to real estate. To put this another way, the dirt-kicking ability and confrontational style appropriate for the adversarial nature of the business are needed. The successful real estate investment practitioner may have more the mentality of a corporate raider than the mindset of the traditional money manager.

WINNER'S GAME STRATEGY

The implications for the serious investor in a market characterized by infrequent transactions, expensive information, limited comparability of investments, and many market participants who are unsophisticated and casual in their approach, are profound. These conditions contribute to market inefficiencies and in turn both create the opportunity for extraordinary investment results and impose the imperative of proceeding with caution. Transference of investing styles that have worked in the corporate securities markets is, as noted at the outset of this article, a perilous proposition.

The real estate market is a very different game from corporate securities. The dimensions and surface of the playing fields have many differences, and the rules and competitive thrusts are less common than similar. If corporate securities investing can be considered a loser's game, then real estate investing should be considered a winner's game. The implication of this different game theory perspective is that the rewards for superior capabilities and expertise are greater in real estate, and simultaneously, the penalties for miscalculation and marginal competence are greater.

Expertise merits a greater premium in real estate investing than it does in most corporate investing settings. At the same time, the skills of the professional securities analyst and investment manager are readily adaptable to the real estate setting, provided the appropriate adjustments are made and the requisite knowledge is obtained. If properly pursued, strategy transference from a loser's game to a winner's game can be a winning proposition. Such strategies for real estate, however, must reflect an understanding of the games that the stock market didn't teach you.

The Challenge of Performance Measurement and the Choice of Management Techniques

Blake Eagle

Real estate people frequently cite impressive rates of return when promoting real estate investments. Claims that real estate has outperformed one or another asset class are common. However, meaningful and accurate historical data on real estate investment returns are not readily available. In fact, real estate performance measurement is at about the same stage today as stock market measurement was at the beginning of this century or bond portfolio measurement was 25 years ago. Those closely involved with real estate performance measurement fully recognize the complexities involved in measuring returns to real estate investing. Most would agree that much work remains to be done.

PROBLEMS IN MEASURING REAL ESTATE PERFORMANCE

Real estate is the most ancient and most universal form of investment. Returns to investments in real estate are the most difficult of all of the major asset classes to measure. The problems in measuring real estate investment performance are well recognized by industry professionals. Transfers of real estate are frequently the result of private negotiations. Consequently, accurate transaction prices are difficult to obtain and monitor. Even if price information is known, the data may not be useful unless the properties are comparable and the transaction details are similar.

Unlike the more efficient stock and bond markets, the real estate market is characterized by the lack of a free flow of information. Worse, the information that is available may not be reliable. In fact, sometimes it is in the real estate practitioner's best interest to release misinformation to keep competitors at bay. The absence of complete, accurate, and reliable information is a classic example of an inefficient marketplace. The active participants in real estate markets—developers, builders, promoters, brokers, entrepreneurs—seek to capitalize on the market's inefficiencies.

Structural Changes in Real Estate Financing

For the better part of this century, the marketplace has been characterized by developers and investors who built, developed, and/or transacted using money borrowed from a financial institution—a life insurance company, bank, or thrift—at a fixed rate, secured by the property, and paid back in level installments over a 25- to 30-year period. The developer/entrepreneur sought capital enhancement through the active role of developing or buying and selling. The passive institutional investor was content to be in a secured position through a bond-like instrument.

The decade of the 1970s introduced a restructuring of real estate capital markets. Two major events—one economic and the other a combination of social and political actions—resulted in altering and realigning the long-standing financial relationships.

The unanticipated high rate of inflation was the first challenge to the previous structure. Inflation clearly impacted the real estate borrower/lender relationships. Long-term borrowers were rewarded handsomely, while the lenders were left holding low fixed-rate mortgages in their portfolios. The American saver was another "loser." During the mid- to late-1970s, property owners were beneficiaries of inflation, since property values maintained purchasing power. Further, growth in property values was magnified when fixed-rate loans were used in financing. Obviously, the traditional relationships could not last. Thus, a high rate of unanticipated inflation was the principal economic event which contributed to the restructuring of the real estate capital market.

Another important event was the enactment

by Congress of ERISA—a massive piece of legislation aimed at establishing fiduciary, vesting, and eligibility standards for the country's private pension system. Among other things, ERISA required that plan assets be adequately diversified in order to protect the plan beneficiaries from being overexposed to any single investment class. To many, this implied that pension fund portfolios should be invested in more asset classes than just stocks and bonds.

ERISA opened the door for U.S. pension funds to become real estate investors. The pool of pension fund assets was expanding rapidly at a time when the real estate industry needed to develop new sources of capital. Further, the nation's private pension systems needed a more inflation-sensitive asset than stocks and bonds. Equity real estate seemed to fit that requirement. Finally, ERISA mandated asset diversification, which implied that fund managers should look beyond traditional financial assets in structuring portfolios. In retrospect, pension funds and the real estate capital market had been on an inevitable collision course.

Need for Real Estate Performance Measurement

During this period, the Frank Russell Company was being asked by our pension consulting clients all of the questions one would expect to hear from passive institutional investors contemplating initial investments in U.S. equity real estate. The questions ranged from "Why should tax-exempt institutions invest in a medium well-known for favoring taxable investors?" to "What kind of real estate properties should be considered by employee benefit plans that exist for only one purpose—to pay promised retirement benefits?" However, the two most frequently asked questions were: "What percentage of plan assets should be invested in property?" and "What have been the asset class historical investment results over time when compared to stocks and bonds?" Trying to answer the asset allocation problem was challenging enough: however, at least there was some precedence for investing plan assets in nontraditional investments. But locating historical performance data on real estate investments was tantamount to finding the proverbial needle in a haystack. Thus, in the early years, pension funds that invested in real estate did so based on the qualitative merits of the asset class.

Qualitative considerations proved to be insufficient justification for expanding real estate commitments in portfolios that previously consisted almost entirely of financial assets. Intuitive beliefs that equity real estate constituted a superior hedge against high rates of unanticipated inflation, that real estate returns were competitive with returns to other asset categories over time, and that real estate could lower overall portfolio volatility were not entirely convincing to investment committees. Quantitative material was needed to support investor intuition. Specifically, a real estate index—the real estate equivalent of the S&P 500—was essential to provide quantitative answers to questions concerning the risks and rewards associated with the addition of equity real estate to pension assets. An index was needed to measure real estate returns over time, in different economic and market environments, and to compare real estate returns to other asset categories. If pension officers and administrators were to convince investment committees to direct money to real estate, they needed quantities of reliable information to support their allocation recommendations. Also, the information must be able to stand the tests of very inquisitive, sometimes skeptical, senior officers and members of the boards of directors.

Developing a Performance Measure

The first attempt to develop quantitative data involved a review of U.S. farm land values. However, data collected by the Department of Agriculture suffered from definitional problems. For example, the USDA might record that Farmer Brown sold his farm to Farmer Jones for $3,000 an acre. But the fact that the property was sold on a 30-year real estate contract at 6 percent was not recorded. By discounting the cash flow to present value, the seller-created financing resulted in the property selling at considerably less than the reported $3,000 per acre. While farm land values could provide a proxy for real estate equity returns, an agricultural data series was not the quantitative answer required to assist pension funds in building a case for real estate. Other data sources examined included FHA lot prices, mortgage interest rates, mortgage capitalization rates, construction cost indexes, labor cost indexes, and materials cost indexes. These series permitted one to draw some conclusions about real estate values in general, but they were merely small, fragmented pieces of a very large and complex puzzle.

In discussing the problem of real estate indexes, Meyer Melnikoff related that he had attempted to attack the problem during the early stages of The Prudential Property Investment Separate Account (PRISA) by reconstructing or extrapolating rates of return using data drawn from Prudential's commercial mortgage portfolio. However, he learned from Prudential's real estate investment department that the information commercial real estate borrowers reported was not of the quality or quantity required to adequately answer challenging questions regarding the validity of any conclusions on performance measurement that would have resulted from this analysis. Meyer also looked into real estate returns in Europe and found that the problems there were just as complex as they were here. He noted that investment performance indexes typically evolve when institutional investors enter new investment markets. Since institutional investors demand reliable information to make investment decisions, they in turn will be a driving force behind the development of performance data bases.

Over the next several months, discussions with real estate managers resulted in a decision to develop a new property-level rate-of-return index. The data base for the new index would be performance information drawn exclusively from their institutionally owned portfolios. These properties possessed several characteristics that made them desirable for use in creating a performance measurement system. Most of the properties had been purchased for all cash. Each portfolio was independently audited. The motivation for acquisition was pure investment. The investors were all tax-exempt, passive institutions who had committed their capital to professional managers who, in turn, invested those dollars in property assets—and in all cases the transactions were at arms length. Further, all the investment managers operated in a fiduciary environment, and the managers employed independent, qualified professional appraisers to estimate market values periodically. Last, but not least, the managers already were reporting performance results on a portfolio basis. Why not take the next step and develop a performance measurement system at the individual property level, thus providing the pension investors with a more detailed measurement and monitoring tool?

In 1977, the Frank Russell Company began asking responsible members of the real estate community, particularly those who worked on behalf of institutional investors in portfolio acquisition and management, to release the information that would allow measurement of real estate investment performance. Some veteran real estate professionals balked at the idea of releasing property information They had been operating successfully without "indexes." However, demands from pension funds for reliable performance measurement data constituted a compelling reason to proceed. After a period of about a year, a group of 14 real estate investment managers agreed "in principle" to the concept.

Through a series of meetings, it became clear that construction of a property-level index was only the first of many promising projects. The accumulation of data for the index project resulted in the formation of the National Council of Real Estate Investment Fiduciaries (NCREIF), a nonprofit organization made up initially of these 14 real estate managers. The goal of NCREIF is "to increase the understanding of real estate as an asset class and as an alternative investment vehicle for pension accounts through the use of advanced analytical techniques."

The formation of NCREIF brought together—in one cohesive group—members of the professional real estate community for the sole purpose of responding to the informational needs of pension funds and other passive institutional investors. The FRC Property Index project now had industry authorization and support.

On June 24, 1982, NCREIF and Frank Russell Company jointly announced the formation of the Council and the completion of the development phase of the FRC Property Index. Frank Russell Company collects, verifies, and stores all property data and does all of the Index return calculations and publication. NCREIF members provide the data and through their working subcommittees have established all of the ground rules and procedures for data reporting. The NCREIF accounting committee, comprised of CPAs, has been particularly active, since accurate and precise performance measurement information is the underpinning of the Index.

The FRC Property Index is a first attempt to measure real estate performance. The research committee is now beginning to hammer out the rules for the next index to be constructed to measure participating mortgages. At this point there have not been enough individual participating mortgages originating out of enough individual portfolios to satisfy the academics of the statistical randomness of the investments.

This entire FRC Index data base is under the academic microscope of Professor Mike Miles at the University of North Carolina. It has been academically audited. This is an honest effort by some very deeply concerned and responsible professionals to develop the information required by pension funds.

Performance of the FRC Property Index

The data base had its beginning on December 31, 1977, with 236 properties drawn from approximately 12 portfolios. The dominant portfolios were Equitable, Separate Account Eight, and the Prudential Property Investment Separate Account (PRISA). If we included all of their nonleveraged properties, we would then have had a PRISA-Equitable index. To prevent this, random samples were generated to ensure on a stratified basis that Prudential and Equitable did not overweight the Index data base. The market value at inception was $594 million. As Table 1 shows, on December 31, 1984, there were 918 properties in the data base with a market value of $7.7 billion. This data base can be broken up into a number of different subindexes or matrix-type breakouts.

Table 2 is the distribution of the data base by major property type. At this juncture, office, retail, and industrial are the dominant assets in these portfolios. There are some apartments and hotels. These are generic labels, since office buildings could be subdivided into several different categories, as could the industrial category be subdivided into warehouses, distribution, high-tech, and so forth. This classification represents a starting point in defining different property sectors.

Table 2 also shows where the dollars are invested. With seven years of history we can now look at the patterns of change. Table 3 is the data base by geographical distribution. Figure 1 presents the aggregate index results. The solid line represents the total rate of return of these properties measured quarterly on a time-weighted basis and on a dollar-weighted basis. Thus, big properties have more impact than smaller properties. The dotted line is the income stream, while the dashed line shows the changes in the market value. This one figure, more than

TABLE 1. Data base universe of properties

	Total market/value ($ millions)	Total number of properties
1977		
December 31	$ 594.4	236
1978		
December 31	751.3	295
1979		
December 31	1,258.0	372
1980		
December 31	2,004.5	494
1981		
March 31	2,319.9	528
June 30	2,719.7	570
September 30	3,095.0	623
December 31	3,697.0	682
1982		
March 31	4,120.6	723
June 30	4,515.2	758
September 30	4,692.1	774
December 31	4,905.3	783
1983		
March 31	5,320.5	820
June 30	5,551.5	835
September 30	5,736.2	854
December 31	6,004.8	845
1984		
March 31	6,123.7	837
June 30	6,968.3	900
September 30	7,307.1	904
December 31	7,733.3	918

Source: Frank Russell Company.

anything else, reassures a lot of plan sponsors that real estate is an income-driven asset and that the largest component of return is the income stream. That was hard to understand sometimes during the late 1970s and early 1980s when some incredible real estate returns were being published. But that was a period when rents were going up significantly and future income was being capitalized into the returns. As inflation leveled off, the values also began to level off.

The index measured against some of the other asset class indexes is shown in Figure 2. It shows how real estate has performed over this particular period of time as measured against stock and bond indexes. The line, incidentally, does not deviate much from that on the PRISA report. The difference between the FRC Property Index and the returns of a portfolio such as PRISA is that

TABLE 2. FRC Property Index data base property distribution by type as of December 31, 1984

Property tax	Market value of total index ($ millions)	Market value of properties by percent*	Number of properties	Number of properties by percent
Apartments	$ 245.4	3.2%	21	2.3%
Hotels	191.1	2.5	7	0.8
Industrials	1,976.8	25.6	479	52.2
Offices	3,834.5	49.6	276	30.1
Retail	1,485.4	19.2	135	14.7
Total	$7,733.3	100.0%	918	100.0%

* Total rounded to 100.0 percent.
Source: Frank Russell Company.

TABLE 3. FRC Property Index data base property distribution by geographic region as of December 31, 1984

Region	Market value of total index ($ millions)	Market value of properties by percent	Number of properties	Number of properties by percent
East	$1,775.8	23.0%	125	13.6%
Midwest	1,242.8	16.1	222	24.2
South	2,030.3	26.3	253	27.6
West	2,684.3	34.7	318	34.6
Total	$7,733.3	100.0%	918	100.0%

Source: Frank Russell Company.

FIGURE 1
FRC Property Index (January 1, 1978 through December 31, 1984)

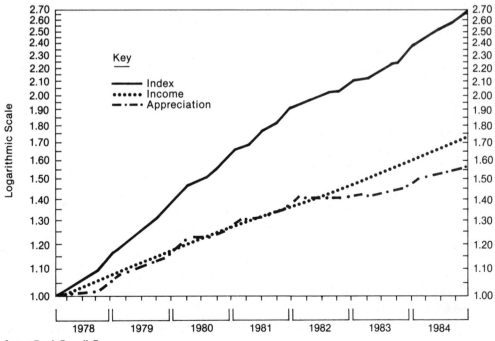

Source: Frank Russell Company.

FIGURE 2
FRC Property Index (January 1, 1978 through December 31, 1984)

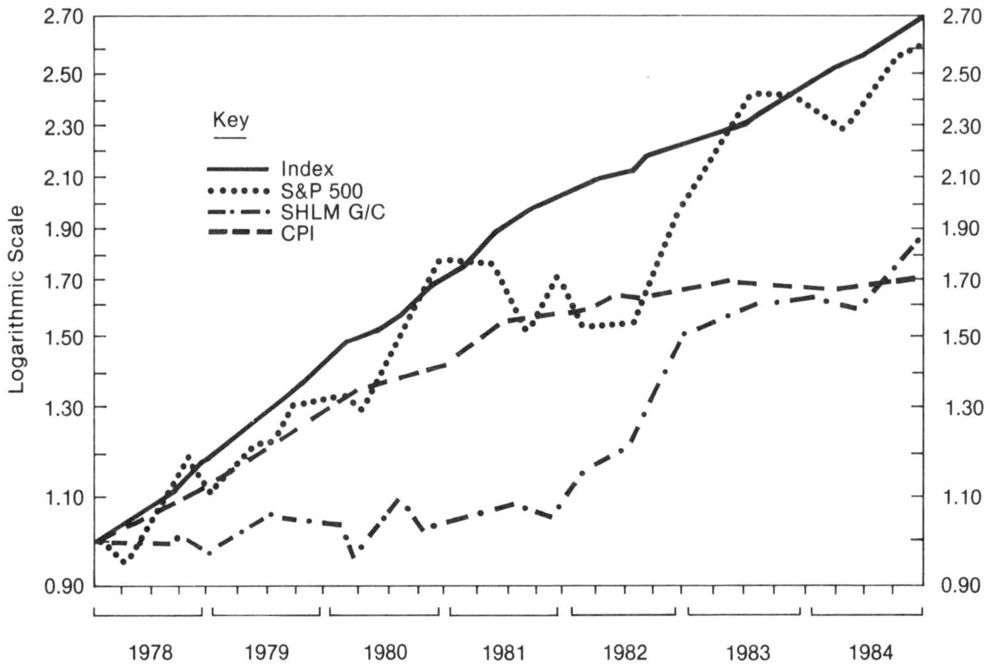

Source: Frank Russell Company.

this is pure property. The PRISA portfolio at times will hold cash, mortgages, other assets, as well as joint ventures and leveraged real estate. All of these investments are a part of PRISA's return. The FRC Property Index is reporting pure property returns.

Tables 4 and 5 present the returns by capital and by income, with each component compounded separately. Note the impact of inflation on appreciation in 1979, 1980, and 1981. You can see where it fell off in 1982 and then starts to come back up again in 1983 and 1984. The annual income stream percentage represents a percentage of the previous year-end market values. This is evidence that commercial real estate values are driven by income.

The data base is broken down by the major property sectors in Table 6. Admittedly there are a very small number of hotels and apartments, but to ignore these assets would not be doing justice to the client. This data base is not aimed at the syndication industry or the retail real estate investment market. The FRC Property Index has been developed for institutional investors to trace investment returns and to help assist in asset allo-cation, as well as to monitor real estate as it is measured against other asset classes.

The individual property sector data can be broken down by income and by appreciation. The sector returns of the different property types can be examined over different time horizons. This information will become even more pertinent and useful as the series is lengthened. Table 7 presents time weighted rates of return on property type subindexes.

One of the criticisms leveled at the appraisal process and at real estate performance measure-ment in general is that real estate market transac-tions do not occur with the frequency or the vol-ume of those in the securities market. While the observation is valid, selling does occur and sales information can be examined for patterns and for comparison to the measures used to report the results in the first place.

Table 8 shows 1984 sales from the FRC Prop-erty Index. Cash of $430 million was received for the sale of 77 properties whose last appraisal was at $418 million. The sales price was $12 mil-lion above the appraised value, or within three percent. Almost 150 properties representing

TABLE 4. FRC Property Index

	Cumulative index values			Annual time-weighted rate of return
	Index	Income	Market value	
1977				
December 31	100.0	100.0	100.0	—
1978				
December 31	115.9	108.7	106.7	15.9%
1979				
December 31	139.8	118.3	118.5	20.6
1980				
December 31	164.8	128.2	129.2	17.9
1981				
March 31	169.6	130.6	130.5	
June 30	176.7	133.3	133.3	
September 30	182.7	135.9	135.3	
December 31	192.2	138.4	139.8	16.6
1982				
March 31	196.9	140.9	140.7	
June 30	200.9	143.6	140.8	
September 30	204.0	146.3	140.3	
December 31	210.1	149.2	141.8	9.3
1983				
March 31	213.6	152.2	141.3	
June 30	219.5	155.2	142.4	
September 30	226.1	157.9	144.2	
December 31	238.0	160.8	149.2	13.3
1984				
March 31	245.0	163.5	151.0	
June 30	253.1	166.5	153.3	
September 30	259.7	169.4	154.6	
December 31	268.8	172.4	157.3	12.9

Source: Frank Russell Company.

nearly $1 billion in gross sales have been sold from the data base in the seven-year period. The variance between the selling price and last appraisal appears to be within 2 percent, based upon preliminary results. Full details concerning the properties sold, including their sales information, the history of appraisal relative to cost, and a complete history of capital improvements have been turned over to the University of North Carolina for intensive study.

TABLE 5. FRC Property Index annual time-weighted rates of return

	1978	1979	1980	1981	1982	1983	1984
Income	8.7%	8.8%	8.4%	8.0%	7.8%	7.8%	7.2%
Capital	6.7	11.1	9.0	8.2	1.4	5.2	5.4
Total	15.9	20.6	17.9	16.6	9.3	13.3	12.9

Note: The income and capital components of return are calculated individually and, thus will not add up to the total annual return because of the effect of cross compounding. These returns have been restated as of first quarter 1984, since previously they were "forced" to add to the total.
Source: Frank Russell Company.

TABLE 6. Property type subindex

	Cumulative index values					
	Index	*Apartments*	*Hotels*	*Industrial*	*Office*	*Retail*
1977						
December 31	100.0	100.0	100.0	100.0	100.0	100.0
1978						
December 31	115.9	116.7	128.1	113.9	121.0	110.5
1979						
December 31	139.8	154.3	222.1	135.5	144.5	124.0
1980						
December 31	164.8	180.7	251.7	157.3	181.3	140.3
1981						
March 31	169.6	184.5	252.5	163.5	187.7	142.4
June 30	176.7	189.9	269.7	169.8	197.9	146.1
September 30	182.7	195.2	274.5	177.2	204.3	150.1
December 31	192.2	205.4	278.5	184.7	218.4	155.7
1982						
March 31	196.9	211.7	290.7	188.6	223.3	158.4
June 30	200.9	220.7	311.9	192.5	228.5	160.6
September 30	204.0	228.1	290.3	197.6	231.9	162.5
December 31	210.1	237.0	307.6	202.6	239.3	166.8
1983						
March 31	213.6	243.0	317.5	206.6	241.7	171.0
June 30	219.5	251.3	328.1	211.5	248.4	176.0
September 30	226.1	260.3	334.9	216.5	256.6	181.9
December 31	238.0	271.4	343.8	230.3	268.5	192.8
1984						
March 31	245.0	280.1	358.2	236.6	276.3	198.5
June 30	253.1	292.6	364.3	243.5	286.1	205.0
September 30	259.7	299.0	370.6	251.1	293.0	210.6
December 31	268.8	303.9	376.9	260.1	301.6	221.7

Source: Frank Russell Company.

TABLE 7. Property type subindex

		Annual time-weighted rates of return				
	Index	*Apartments*	*Hotels*	*Industrial*	*Office*	*Retail*
1978						
Income	8.7%	8.6%	15.1%	8.1%	8.8%	8.2%
Capital	6.7	7.6	11.6	5.4	11.4	2.2
Total	15.9	16.7	28.1	13.9	21.0	10.5
1979						
Income	8.8	8.3	16.1	8.8	8.1	8.8
Capital	11.1	22.6	51.5	9.6	10.7	3.2
Total	20.6	32.3	73.4	19.0	19.4	12.3
1980						
Income	8.4	7.7	11.5	8.5	7.7	8.3
Capital	9.0	8.9	1.6	7.1	16.9	4.5
Total	17.9	17.1	13.3	16.1	25.5	13.1
1981						
Income	8.0	7.6	10.2	8.2	7.3	8.3
Capital	8.2	5.8	0.4	8.6	12.4	2.5
Total	16.7	13.7	10.6	17.4	20.4	11.0
1982						
Income	7.8	7.5	8.6	8.0	7.4	8.6
Capital	1.4	7.5	2.0	1.7	2.1	(1.5)
Total	9.3	15.4	10.5	9.7	9.6	7.1
1983						
Income	7.8	7.1	10.0	7.8	7.2	8.8
Capital	5.2	7.0	1.6	5.5	4.7	6.4
Total	13.3	14.5	11.8	13.7	12.1	15.6
1984						
Income	7.2	6.8	7.2	7.7	6.7	8.1
Capital	5.4	4.9	2.3	4.9	5.4	6.5
Total	12.9	12.0	9.7	12.9	12.4	15.0

Source: Frank Russell Company.

TABLE 8. 1984 total properties sold from FRC Property Index

Sales = 77	
Last appraised M.V.	$418,213,395
Net proceeds	430,445,259
Excess over market	12,231,864

Source: Frank Russell Company.

Eagle Question and Answer Session

QUESTION: Where does the pension fund consultant fit in among the builders, borrowers, and developers?

EAGLE: Our firm focuses strictly on the assets of the pension funds. We help our clients set investment objectives; develop asset allocation parameters; screen, analyze, and review the investment managers; monitor the portfolios; and calculate performance measurement. We represent 40 pension funds whose aggregate assets are close to $100 billion. Our clients, in aggregate, hold more than $10 billion in real estate. We are responsible to our client base for assisting in the selection of their managers and the ongoing measurement of the portfolios, the ongoing understanding of the portfolios and the management organization as well as the dynamics of the marketplace itself. I have colleagues that cover the other asset classes.

QUESTION: What conclusions do you draw from all of this data?

EAGLE: Although our data has been collected for too short a period of time for conclusive analysis, it has shown that investment grade real estate has performed in accordance with expectations.

There is evidence of significant variability in the values of the 150 properties sold from the data base during the seven year history of the Index. The variability is not necessarily correlated with the industry as a whole. While there are properties in this data base that have sold for over $100 million, there are others that have sold for less than $100,000. Some properties have been sold above appraisal, some below, and some have sold exactly at appraisal.

The volatile sector of the market is not the existing high quality sector that is tenanted by American business and industry. It is the unfinanced sector, the speculative development sector, and where individuals or groups have made significant heavy bets in a single property sector or a single location and where the economics of real estate have not been the investment motivation. If I have learned anything in 14 years of being a pension consultant, it is that the professional managers have demonstrated to me their knowledge of the marketplace, its dynamics and

how to invest. Their successes have far overshadowed their mistakes. The most critical decision that a pension fund has to make beyond real estate allocation is who to hire as their investment management team.

QUESTION: Blake, can a pension fund sponsor use the FRC Property Index as the minimum acceptable long-term performance for measuring real estate investment managers?

EAGLE: It really should not be used to measure a manager unless you have equal time periods and comparable assets in order to have an apples versus apples comparison. This is one of the concerns that we have about an index of this type— that it is being used to measure someone's apples with someone else's oranges. There are plenty of ways to measure one manager against the other because in the pension world the managers have to publish their performance results anyway. We would rather have this index used for allocation, for academic research, and to see how real estate stacks up both against the other asset classes over time and against itself in different market cycles. So I would not encourage this to be used for measuring a manager, though I happen to know that it is used for that.

QUESTION: What key statistics ought to be presented on a regular basis to investors to illustrate performance—yields on cost, yields on value, internal rates of return, before or after debt service?

EAGLE: The key to real estate is the income stream, and the definition of investment grade real estate is the quality, consistency, and durability of the income stream. And that income stream measured against cost or market value is the basis upon which values are obtained. You just have to take it on an asset by asset basis. This data base is representative of the high quality sector of income-producing real estate.

QUESTION: What are you doing about measuring risk?

EAGLE: Well, the sales will give us the opportunity to measure the variability of individual assets and that is now under study at the University of North Carolina.

Real Estate Development: Investment Risks and Rewards

Joseph W. O'Connor

The purpose of this paper is to discuss some of the risks and rewards associated with investing in real estate development. Of the $4.5 billion real estate portfolio that Copley Real Estate Advisors manages today, about 90 percent has been involved in real estate development in one fashion or another. It is a real estate investment strategy in which we have specialized.

An analysis of the risks and rewards in real estate development requires that several questions be addressed. How does a developer create value in property? What are the profit margins and what are the risks? To answer these questions, a 20-year statistical analysis of development risks and rewards has been compiled from a real estate portfolio that includes $2 billion of developmental properties.

THE DEVELOPMENT PROCESS

The development process is outlined in Figure 1. The horizontal axis represents a 36-month time frame in which the six stages of development and property ownership are shown; six distinct functions that need to be undertaken in developing any property.

The first stage is planning and design. This includes supply and demand considerations, a market analysis, and some proforma representation of expected performance. In other words, if this building is built in this market, given anticipated supply and demand, can a profit be expected? Does this project have a reasonable return on its cost?

The second phase generally involves obtaining the necessary regulatory approvals. In some markets, such as Houston, regulatory approvals can be obtained in a few weeks; in some other markets, such as Boston, it can be a period of years or even decades. The elements of financing, construction, and leasing are next. Last, but not least, is the operational phase. Most investors get involved only in the operational phase of real estate investing. They buy completed, leased buildings at a 9 percent cash yield. Certain institutional investors, however, integrate backward along this development line; they are willing to take different risk positions in different markets at different times.

For example, given the strength of the industrial marketplace in many areas of the United States today, Copley is willing to assume signifi-

FIGURE 1
The development process

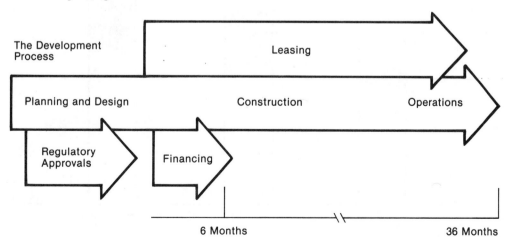

Source: Copley Real Estate Advisors.

cant leasing risk in industrial projects, yet in other areas we will not assume any risk. Developmental investors manage risk by taking different positions in different markets at different points in time depending upon their analysis of the supply/demand equation, the development risks, and the available profit margins

INVESTMENT STRATEGIES AND EXPECTED RETURNS

When a real estate investor projects real estate yields, three critical factors are considered. The first is cash-on-cash yield, the second is the effect of inflation and/or economic growth on the property's income stream, and the third is the property's projected residual value. Inflation of rents and cash flow is largely outside the control of individual investors. Similarly, residual value is to a large extent controlled by changes in inflation and reproduction costs. Cash-on-cash yield, on the other hand, can be more readily controlled utilizing different investment strategies. Cash yields, the area where real estate advisors can have the most significant impact for clients, is the primary focus.

Three strategies employed by investors in today's real estate marketplace are shown in Figure 2. The first strategy, buy and hold, invests in completed, fully leased income producing property on an unleveraged basis. The lower segment represents the expected first year yield. It indicates that an unleveraged property investment in today's market should have a 9 percent cash yield. That's the cash from a property that an investor can put in his pocket each year. Given a 5 percent inflation expectation, a 14 percent discounted yield might be projected.

The second strategy employs a "hybrid" real estate investment structure where the investor assumes some lease-up risk and has a higher cash yield, maybe 10.5 or 11 percent, and a discounted yield of 14 to 16 percent.

The third strategy, "real estate development," would generally have a 12.5 or 13 percent annual cash yield, and a discounted yield before leverage of about 17 or 18 percent.

A typical profile for a $10 million development commitment is shown in Figure 3. In this example a completed, fully leased office building with a 9 percent cash yield would have a value of about $10 million in the marketplace. How-

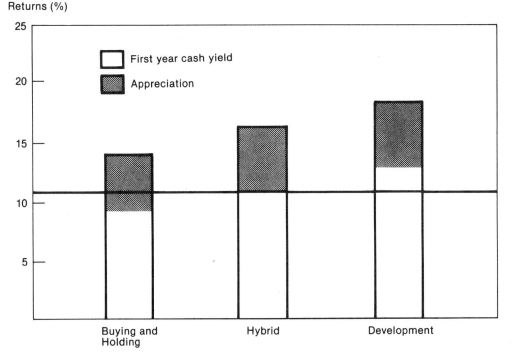

FIGURE 2
Expected nominal returns

Annual
Returns (%)

Source: Copley Real Estate Advisors.

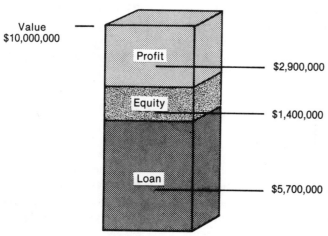

FIGURE 3
Imputed development profit

Value $10,000,000

Profit — $2,900,000

Equity — $1,400,000

Loan — $5,700,000

Source: Copley Real Estate Advisors.

ever, based on current development profit margins, the actual cost of developing that asset over 18 to 24 months would be about $7.1 million. This indicates that you can build at a 12.5 percent cash yield and sell at a 9 percent cash yield; the difference provides a very substantial profit margin.

This figure also shows that many developmental investors use outside leverage to enhance returns. In this particular example, $1.4 million of equity is used to build a $10 million building which should have about $2.5 to $3.0 million of developmental profit when completed and leased. When assessing financial risk in developmental situations, it's important to realize that the $2.5 to $3.0 million of profit can be accessed before impairing invested capital.

DEVELOPMENT RISK AND REWARDS

There are two currently held theories concerning the risks in real estate development. The first was expressed in a January 1985 article, "Real Estate Development: How much risk can you take?" The author, a prominent real estate investment advisor, wrote that a long-term developmental investment program is made up of spectacular successes and spectacular failures. In other words, development is a roll of the dice.

The other theory, adopted by most real estate developers, is that the high profit margins in real estate development always cover the developmental risk in new investments. Our actual experience during the last two decades has been somewhere between those two theories.

In order to quantify risk in developmental investing, data from a real estate portfolio that Copley has been managing for 20 years was examined. Every single developmental property with an operating history was included. The sample consisted of 40 properties, about $2.0 billion of assets, and 23 million square feet of space developed since 1967. The goal was to analyze the volatility of returns in that portfolio. How variable were the critical risk components of each project? Was the uncertainty in construction and lease-up adequately rewarded by consistently higher returns? How different were actual cash-on-cash yields from the projections?

The internal rate of return analysis on all 40 of these investments range from a low of −5 percent up to investments that have internal rates of return approaching 60, 70, and 80 percent. (See Figure 4.) This represents the return to the investor; the return to the joint venture partner is on top of that. The horizontal axis indicates the year the development was started.

This portfolio is a good sample. It represents a significant investment portfolio with a substantial number of properties, about 500 individual buildings constructed in 100 different phases of development. Twenty-two developers created these properties in 12 different states over the last 17 years in good and bad markets and in

FIGURE 4
Internal rate of return analysis on 40 developmental properties

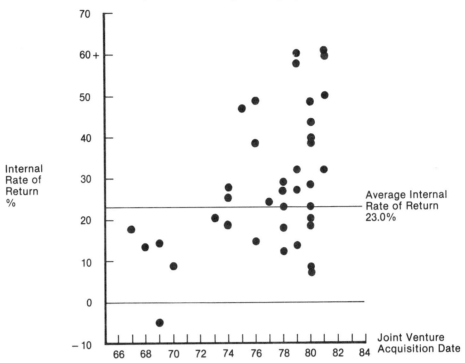

Source: Copley Real Estate Advisors.

times of both high and low inflation. Each investment is at least 4 years old, with an average age of 7.7 years. The sample does have two limiting factors. First, it is a portfolio that was managed by just one investment advisor with a very specific investment strategy. Second, as a result of the sample's specificity, it lacks a few real estate components. It does not include any residential properties, any large mixed-use complexes, or any large downtown high rise office buildings. However, on balance, for the assessment of risk in a specific developmental investment portfolio, it is a good sample.

As shown in Figure 4, there was an actual loss of capital on a developmental investment in 3 percent of the cases. An additional 7 percent of the sample yielded returns below what could have been obtained in a safe investment, a high grade corporate bond for example. However, 90 percent of the time the portfolio exceeded its alternative safe investment yield. In addition, this large, diversified portfolio built over the last 20 years had a consolidated internal rate of return of 23 percent and exceeded the expected return

of a so called "safe" real estate project 85 percent of the time.

The next step was to take a specific group of joint ventures and examine their performance on a more detailed basis. Where were the risks in their development and how did actual volatility compare to expected volatility? These 18 joint ventures, shown as lighter dots on Figure 5, have a consolidated average internal rate of return over 17 years of 24 percent versus 23 percent for the entire sample. The 18 joint ventures also show geographical diversification (9 states) and age (8.3 years average) similar to the larger portfolio. These 18 developments were built in 47 different phases over the last 17 years. In total, it is still an extremely large, diverse sample constituting nearly $1.4 billion of assets.

As mentioned earlier, initial cash-on-cash yield as shown below, is the most important determinant as to whether one profits by assuming the risks of real estate development. Comparable quality property can be bought at a 9 percent yield in the marketplace. The difference between that 9 percent and what can be earned on a devel-

FIGURE 5
Internal rate of return analysis on 18 joint ventures

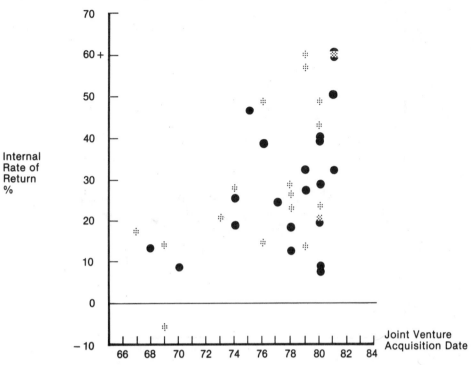

Source: Copley Real Estate Advisors.

opmental investment represents "profit" for the risk taken.

Cash-on-cash yield is simply net cash flow divided by total development cost.

$$\text{Cash-on-Cash} = \frac{\text{Net Cash Flow}}{\text{Total Development Cost}}$$

In assessing the risks in obtaining higher cash-on-cash yields, the volatility of the denominator, total costs, was examined. How do costs vary in this sample? Where were the cost overruns and where were we on budget? Was it in shell cost, the cost of the physical structure? Tenant improvements? Or soft costs (i.e., interest expense during development and lease-up costs)?

After assessing the volatility in costs, the actual net income must be examined. These two components, income and cost, determine yield. When an investment is approved, before the first spade goes into the ground, estimates of income and total cost are compiled. In the following analysis, the difference between forecast and actual values for the 47 different phases of the 18 development samples were carefully examined. By quantifying the variance from the original best

estimate, the risks of investing in real estate development can be assessed. It is again important to realize that these 47 projects were built over the last 2 decades in both good and bad real estate markets in periods of both high and low inflation.

Now for the results. Shell costs, the cost of constructing the basic building shell, are shown in the scatter diagram in Figure 6, showing the percentage variance of shell cost from projections. A positive (+) variance means costs exceeded expectations. In 95 percent of the cases, actual costs were within ±10 percent of the projection. The mean variance is 1.8 percent. That is, over 17 years in more than a $1 billion worth of development, shell cost was missed, on average, by 2 percent. The volatility is quite limited and that is to be expected. These are fairly simple office, R&D, and industrial buildings with uncomplicated construction built over relatively short periods of time.

Variance in tenant improvement cost is shown in Figure 7. The greater variability results from the inability to obtain firm prices for tenant improvements prior to the start of construction; tenant improvement cost is determined by each

FIGURE 6
Percentage variance of cost of constructing the basic building shell

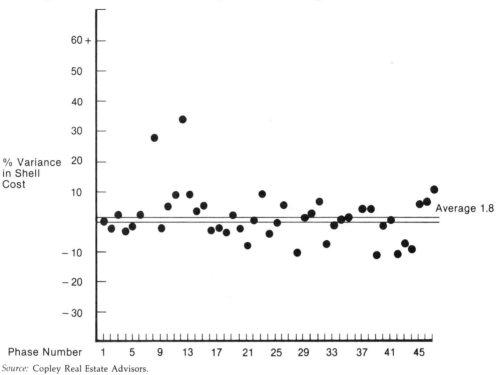

Source: Copley Real Estate Advisors.

FIGURE 7
Variance in tenant improvement cost

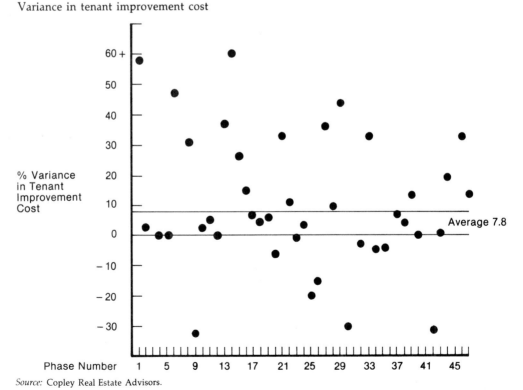

Source: Copley Real Estate Advisors.

tenant's needs. However in reviewing these data, positive variances—high increases in tenant improvement costs—are not necessarily bad. In many instances there is a direct correlation between extra improvements and higher rental income. The variability is significant; actual costs were 7.8 percent over budget, on average, for tenant improvements.

Variance in soft costs from budget is shown in Figure 8. Soft costs are primarily interest expense during lease-up and some marketing costs. Although one would expect a fair amount of volatility in soft costs, on average a favorable variance of 6.2 percent was experienced. Soft costs were 6 percent less than anticipated at the time the investment was approved.

Results for the total cost component of the cash-on-cash equation are summarized in Figure 9. In effect, this sums the three previous cost components. It shows that 93 percent of the sample was within ±10 percent of the projected estimate of total cost. More importantly, on average, the 47 phases of these 18 developments constructed over a 17-year period came in at one percent under their originally expected total cost.

Next, what is the net cash flow from the leas-

ing of these properties relative to the anticipated value? Figure 10 shows that 4 percent of the sample was significantly below projected net operating income, while 53 percent of the sample clusters between 0 and 15 percent above the net operating income expected when the project was started. Overall, net operating income had a positive variance of 13.2 percent.

The most important issue is, what happens to these individual components as expressed by the variance in cash-on-cash yields? Figure 11 describes the variance in actual cash-on-cash yields in the 47 investment sample. In 9 situations (i.e., 19 percent of the sample) the cash-on-cash yields were lower than anticipated. However, 81 percent of the developments had cash yields equal to or greater than their initial projections, and the whole portfolio had cash-on-cash yields 15 percent higher, on average, than anticipated.

To put this in perspective, the actual cash-on-cash yields, not just the variances, should be examined. The actual cash-on-cash yields, 15.7 percent on average on an unleveraged basis, are shown in Figure 12. Assuming a property can be sold at a 9 percent yield, there clearly has been a substantial increase in value during the

FIGURE 8
Variance in soft costs

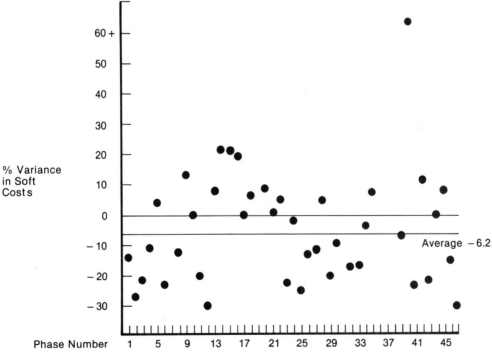

Source: Copley Real Estate Advisors.

FIGURE 9
Total cost component of the cash-on-cash equation

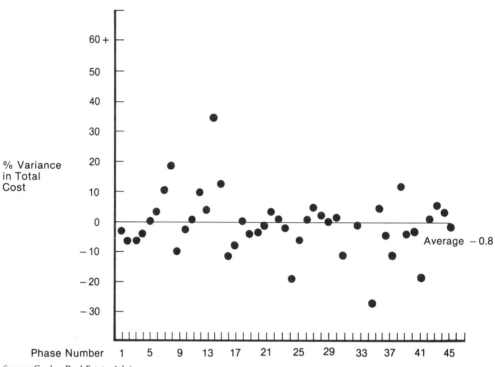

Source: Copley Real Estate Advisors.

FIGURE 10
Variance in net cash flow relative to the anticipated value

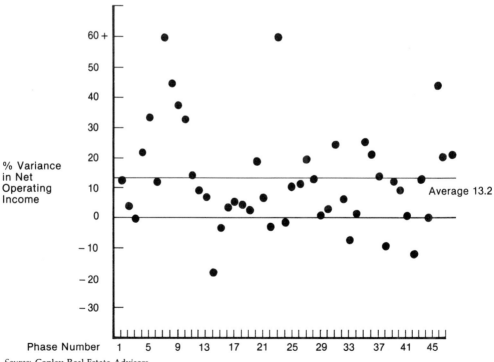

Source: Copley Real Estate Advisors.

FIGURE 11
Variance in actual cash-on-cash yields

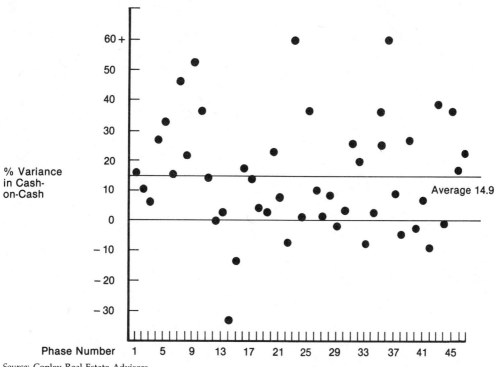

Source: Copley Real Estate Advisors.

FIGURE 12
Actual cash-on-cash yields

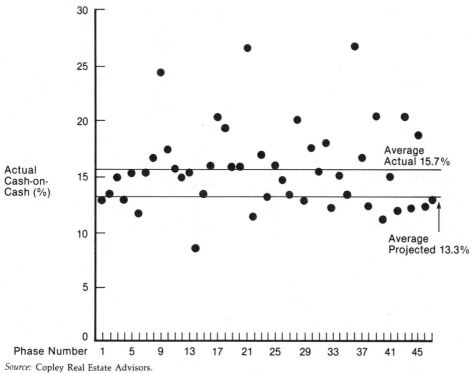

Source: Copley Real Estate Advisors.

FIGURE 13
FRC Property Index (January 1, 1978–June 30, 1984)

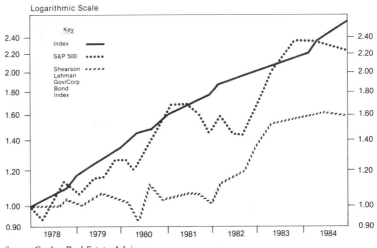

Source: Copley Real Estate Advisors.

development period. Although there has been a significant amount of volatility in a number of key areas, the end result has been a portfolio that met or exceeded expectations 80 percent of the time. The standard deviation on these actual cash-on-cash yields is 3.8 percent. Even moving down two standard deviations, actual cash-on-cash yield would be about 9 percent on the low side, which is what one would expect to pay to buy a property today.

In summary, the risk factors in this portfolio have been in lease-up, the area that concerns most everyone today, and not in hard construction costs. This analysis suggests that there is not as much risk if development is done on a dollar cost averaging basis in relatively small buildings over long periods of time with professional development partners. The overall variances have been much more favorable than one might initially anticipate. Certainly there has been somewhat more volatility in returns in this portfolio than in an unleveraged nondevelopmental portfolio. That risk, however, has been extremely well rewarded in a large portfolio over a long period of time. The study indicates a 900 to 1,000 basis points yield advantage over the standard real estate portfolio.

Figure 13 displays the Frank Russell Property Index beginning in January, 1978. It's important to note that this is a log chart, a straight line represents a constant rate of return. The real estate line, an aggregate of several unleveraged nondevelopmental portfolios, consistently shows less volatility than the S&P 500 and the Shearson

Lehman Bond Index. Strictly on a return basis, this index indicates that over the last seven years $1.00 invested in real estate on an unleveraged basis in 1978 would have a value of $2.40 today.

Based on the entire portfolio of 40 investments with an average compounded annual return of 23 percent, $1.00 invested in that developmental portfolio in 1978 would have a value of $4.25 in 1984. These are historic returns and it is a tougher marketplace today; margins are probably going to shrink. This example does indicate, however, the spread between nondevelopmental returns and developmental returns. The $1.00 invested in unleveraged real estate in 1978 grew by $1.40 in seven years, while $1.00 invested in leveraged developmental real estate in 1978 increased in value by $3.25. The difference, $1.85 of profit on that original $1.00 invested, represents the investment premium for assuming the risks of real estate development.

CONCLUSION

Our experience has been that the risks associated with real estate development have been lower than many would assume. Historically, investors have been well-rewarded for investing in real estate development. Future real estate markets are expected to be more difficult and development profit margins are expected to shrink. Overall, however, there is a good case to be made for investing in real estate development. Based on our experience, that risk has been well rewarded over the last 20 years.

Timberland Investment— A Viable Alternative

Robert G. Chambers

There is little doubt that long-term real estate investments will play an increasingly important role in investment portfolios. Other speakers have documented past growth and projected future increases in the real estate component of investment portfolios. The purpose of this paper is to present the case for including timberland in the real estate component of a diversified portfolio.

OPPORTUNITIES IN SOUTHERN TIMBERLAND

In today's depressed forest economy significant opportunities are present for investments in West Coast timber. Although we would not discourage such investments, one must be aware of the higher associated risk. Opportunities also exist for northeastern timberland, but this potential is in the long-term future. We believe the South is the place for portfolio diversification with minimum risk. Three observations lead to this position.

First, southern pine timber is rapidly becoming a scarce economic commodity since demand is increasing faster than supply. Max Peterson, Chief of the United States Forest Service recently stated:

> Just a little more than half a lifetime away, the United States will have a total of over 300 million people, 30 percent more than today. Each individual's purchasing power will nearly triple, while disposable personal income will nearly quadruple.

The U.S. Forest Service projects that, in the same period, 19 million acres of forest land, an area the size of South Carolina, will be taken out of timber production. This land will be converted to nontimber uses, such as residential areas, right-of-ways, and shopping centers. The lost areas will come from the most productive land, and most of the loss will occur in the South according to the U.S. Forest Service.

The U.S. Forest Service concludes that "Demands are rising faster than supplies. Thus, the outlook is one of increasing economic scarcity with rising timber prices."

Second, the forest industry will continue to expand at a much faster rate in the South than in the nation as a whole. The reason for this is twofold: first, the population of the South and West is expected to increase by 31 percent and 45 percent respectively, while the population in the Midwest and Northeast is expected to decline by 4 percent; second, the western forest, mostly owned by the government and heavily regulated, will not be able to respond to the increasing demand. The South, therefore, will continue to increase its market share of forest products manufacturing.

Third, the current soft market for southern pine timber is the result of high interest rates which dampen domestic demand and a strong dollar which reduces export opportunities. We are experiencing a classic cash buyer's market for timberland and are excited at the opportunities being offered.

TIMBERLAND INVESTMENT PHILOSOPHY

The investment philosophy, which recognizes timberland as a uniquely attractive long-term investment, may be stated in four points:

- Timberland investments will generate attractive total returns relative to other investments with little risk.
- Timberland investment provides plan sponsors with an opportunity to achieve better diversification and thus reduce overall portfolio risk.
- Timberland has demonstrated an ability to provide investors with a hedge against inflation and to produce real rates of return.
- Timberland offers visible growth year after year which contributes directly to the increasing value of the asset itself.

These advantages make a compelling argument for the inclusion of timberland in a long-term investment portfolio.

TIMBERLAND INVESTMENT STRATEGY

There are three sources of value increase in a timberland investment: land appreciation, timber price appreciation, and biological growth. (See Table 1.) Investments in timberland may be structured so as to maximize the benefit from each of the sources of value increase.

Land Appreciation

The U.S. Forest Service has projected that land will appreciate in value at a rate of from zero to 2 percent per year in real terms.

The market value of land is defined as the price a willing buyer will pay and a willing seller will accept, both being reasonably informed and neither being under duress. Even if one is not trying to sell a property, the appraised value is assumed to be equal to a comparable property which has, in fact, recently sold.

The greatest impetus to land value is the competition caused by a large number of potential buyers. Smaller properties, which we have defined as from 200 to 5,000 acres in size, have a larger universe of potential buyers simply because more buyers can afford them. This larger universe will generate competition and consequently increase the value of smaller timberland properties.

Good access and high productive capacity will also add to buyer interest and increase the number of potential buyers for a particular property, thus increasing land values.

Timber Price Appreciation

The U.S. Forest Service has projected that timber prices will appreciate in real terms at the rate of 2 to 4 percent per year.

Long-term timber price trends are influenced primarily by world economic conditions. Our basic premise in timberland investments is that long-term world markets are favorable.

Short-term timber price fluctuations are influenced by species, local market conditions, timber product class, and the accessibility and ease

TABLE 1. Sources for potential appreciation (real rates)

Item	Low	Medium	High
Land appreciation*	0.0%	1.0%	2.0%
Timber appreciation*	2.0	3.0	4.0
Timber growth†	2.0	4.0	6.0
First Atlanta's goal: 6%–9% Real			

* U.S. Forest Service.
† Morgan Stanley & Company.

with which a particular timberland property can be harvested.

An investment strategy should be based on southern pine, the most sought after and valuable species in the South and one of the most important timber species in the nation.

The major factors influencing short-term prices for southern pine are local market conditions and the product class offered for sale in the existing market. The impact of local market conditions is evident by looking at current price differentials in the South as shown by Table 2.

You will note significant differences in the three market areas which we have identified. There is a wide spread in pulpwood prices, ranging from $17 to $32 per cord. Pine chip-n-saw exhibits less differential, while pine sawtimber, much like pulpwood, exhibits substantial differences.

The second major determinant of price is the product class being sold. Sawtimber is more valuable than pulpwood.

Timber prices also vary for each product class within a given area, depending upon tree quality and the ease with which the trees can be harvested and transported to the mill. Better quality trees will always sell for a higher price than poorer quality ones. Trees located in areas with good access to public roads are more valuable than inaccessible ones. Trees on well-drained soil, located next to a good public road will always command a premium price during extended periods of wet weather.

The ability to respond to short-term changes in local timber markets can also be strengthened by developing relationships with consulting for-

TABLE 2. Price differential by zone (dollar/cord)

Product	Zone 1	Zone 2	Zone 3
Pine pulpwood	$32	$17	$19
Pine chip-n-saw	55	45	45
Pine sawtimber	60	55	52

esters in local areas. Many consulting firms throughout the South have been operating in their respective areas for more than 30 years. These firms have each sold millions of board feet of timber and participated in the acquisition and management of literally millions of acres of southern pine timberland. A relationship with consultants will strengthen an investor's presence in local timber markets.

While these strategies will maximize the contribution of land and timber price appreciation, investors cannot affect the rate of appreciation. That rate is determined by economic factors that no single owner can influence. The best one can do is attempt to understand the influences and maximize their contribution to the portfolio.

Timber Growth

Biological growth of timber, the largest source of appreciation in a timberland portfolio, can be controlled directly by the portfolio manager. The fact that biological growth is independent of economic forces is tremendously exciting. Neither downward nor upward price trends have any direct effect on timber growth. A forest manager can plan, direct, and control the largest and most consistent source of value appreciation in a timberland portfolio.

To further emphasize this point—one can buy the most productive land in the South, with the best access and located in areas with the strongest markets. Yet in prolonged economic downturns, even with the assistance of the strongest consultants, land and timber prices will decline. At the same time, timber growth is maintained and mitigates some, if not all, of the negative forces resulting from economic downturns.

When prices increase, they increase on both the amount purchased plus the amount grown. This is shown by the example in Table 3. For simplification this example considers only the pine portion of the portfolio.

One should remember that the same forces affect the total portfolio, including both pine and hardwood products. Note that even with a 2 percent decline in timber prices the portfolio will yield a real rate of return of 1.88 percent. Very few investments can yield real rates of return while experiencing a decline in the per-unit-value of the portfolio. Table 3 illustrates that biological growth offsets decreases in timber prices and magnifies increases.

TABLE 3. Impact of timber growth on a timber investment

Price change (percent)	Real (percent)
−2	1.88
0	3.56
+2	6.08

The phenomenon of biological growth of timber provides a real rate of increase under a wide array of economic conditions. The truly significant impact of biological growth can best be seen by studying a typical growth curve as shown in Figure 1. There are two forces being exhibited in this growth curve. First, trees, being their own factory, become larger and therefore contain more volume each year. For example, we are currently growing approximately five million board feet of sawtimber each year in our timberland portfolio. This growth rate will increase as we continue to implement our management strategy.

Second, as trees become larger, they change product classes and their total volume becomes more valuable. This phenomenon, called ingrowth, is shown in Table 4. As a forest grows, it produces more units, each becoming more valuable.

Quite obviously, by combining rapid biological growth with ingrowth into larger, more valuable produce classes, one can significantly enhance the real rate of increase in the value of a timberland portfolio.

As an example, why buy a 25-year-old sawtimber tree at the top of its growth curve? It will only grow about 4 percent and is currently in the highest value product class. It will not become more valuable by growing larger. This strategy would rely on price appreciation for performance.

The more prudent approach is to buy premerchantable pine and capture the most rapid biological growth in the life of the tree. Then watch your investment grow from low-value pulpwood, to moderate-value chip-n-saw, and finally to more valuable sawtimber.

As we have outlined, a timberland invest-

TABLE 4. Ingrowth of timber

Age	Total units per acre	Value per unit	Value per acre
14	16.0	$37	$1,117.80
20	50.9	39	2,001.50
25	58.2	41	2,388.20

FIGURE 1
Typical growth curve

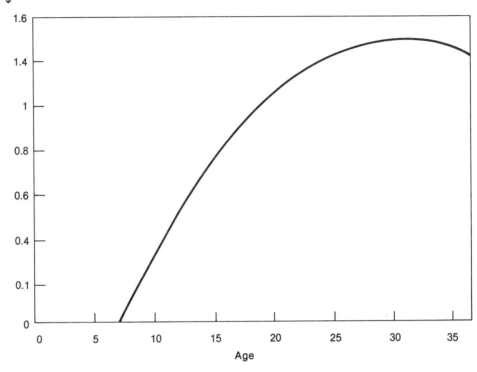

ment strategy may be designed to maximize the contribution of land appreciation, timber price appreciation, and timber growth.

CHARACTERISTICS OF ACQUISITION ZONES

There is one additional important function that an investment strategy can perform. We can minimize the volatility of the performance of a timberland portfolio by recognizing the unique contribution each source of appreciation makes in different regions of the South.

Three acquisition zones with unique investment characteristics can be identified.

Zone 1 is an area of relatively stable high prices for forest products. The timberland in this area has a higher productive potential on the average than other acres of the South. In this zone, the combination of high productive capacity and relatively stable high prices will yield very favorable returns. We suggest that 15 percent of a timberland portfolio be invested in this zone.

Zone 2 is an area of moderate timber prices and average to better-than-average site quality. This area has the greatest potential for price increases because of the expansion of the local forest industry. We suggest that 70 percent of a timberland portfolio be invested in Zone 2.

Zone 3 is an area of relatively low market price. Therefore, this zone has the potential for the greatest price increases. We recommend that 15 percent of a timberland portfolio be invested in Zone 3.

TIMBERLAND PORTFOLIO MANAGEMENT

After a timberland property is acquired, a management plan may be written to maximize the annual rate of increase in the value of the portfolio. Foresters often get caught in the trap of discussing whether the prudent investor should

FIGURE 2
Typical rate of return

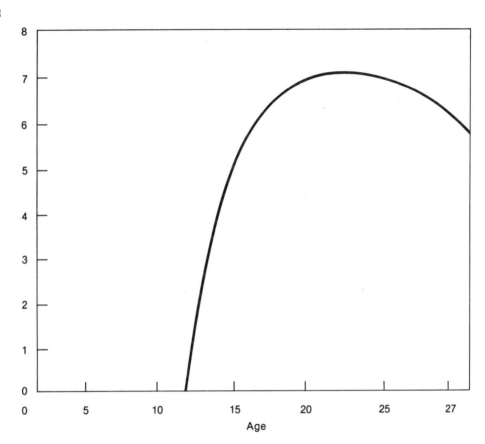

ROR
%

Age

grow pulpwood, sawlogs, or other products. The emphasis should be on growing money, that is, to maximize the rate of return on the investment. Most clients have the same goal.

Consider again the typical growth curve, this time expressed as the annual compound rate of increase since acquisition as shown in Figure 2. Note that the compound rate of return peaks at a fairly early age. This is the point at which the timber should be removed from the portfolio.

The forest management plan may be implemented by:

- Immediately installing prudent management practices to control risk of biological loss, for example, installing fire protection barriers and conducting prescribed burning.
- Immediately plant genetically improved pine seedlings on open areas.
- Implement plans to maximize biological growth rates by harvesting mature, slow-

growing stands and reenter the growth curve by investing in young trees.

Each timber harvest must meet the following criteria:

- The harvest must be sold at a unique time to protect the initial investment price. Fortunately, timber can be stored, or warehoused, on the stump in the forest to wait out downturns in stumpage values or for premium prices during prolonged periods of wet weather.
- The harvest must result in a regenerated stand which will increase the rate of growth of the investment when reinvestment in replanting is considered.
- Tracts that do not meet the criteria for timber harvest should be aggressively marketed in an effort to remove them from the portfolio

and thereby increase the quality of the total portfolio.

CONCLUSION

Timberland today is at about the same place as conventional equity real estate was ten years ago. During the last ten years real estate assets held by investors experienced a dramatic rate of growth. Even with today's investment levels, equity real estate has a long way to go because of the enormous future growth projected for all asset classes of U.S. pension funds. We believe timberland will share in this growth.

The Practical Problems of Long-Term Real Estate Investing

David P. Feldman

AT&T's Pension Fund is committed to real estate investment for the following reasons: (1) the asset is viewed as an excellent inflation hedge; (2) it offers significant diversification potential; (3) the returns on real estate properties are negatively correlated with returns to stocks and bonds; and (4) it offers stability of returns.

AT&T's DIVESTITURE CHALLENGE

Divestiture created an unusual challenge for the Bell System and AT&T, particularly on the real estate front. It meant, among other things, pension assets had to be split into nine pieces. Real estate posed some very particular problems, as it is a unique asset and not easily divisible. We decided to set up a closed-end real estate trust of about $4 billion, with the divested Regional Operating Companies and Bell Communications Research. The establishment of the trust centralized work for all the participants by owning units in it. The trust has a limited life. Since we can buy and sell units among each other, anyone wanting to pursue another avenue has an opportunity to cash in units for the appraised value, if cash is available from the remaining participants. Since January 1, 1984, while we remained the overall manager for the $4 billion in the real estate investments made on behalf of the Bell System, each of the Regional Operating Companies is going its own way and will be setting its own forward-looking real estate policies.

AT&T'S INVESTMENT PHILOSOPHY AND APPROACH

Because real estate is a very opportunistic business, we set up some objectives early on at AT&T. In terms of property, we looked into office, retail, industrial, residential, hotel, and raw land as likely categories, trying to determine what was available in the market and what seemed reasonable from a risk/return standpoint.

A portfolio that is reasonably balanced in terms of geographical location of properties is important. We had our own set of guidelines for the geographical distribution of properties in the East, West, Midwest, and South. We adopted the regional classification of the National Council of Real Estate Investment Fiduciaries (NCREIF). We were balanced within our own system, but it is still balanced overall in terms of geography with NCREIF.

In terms of investment type we established objectives for commingled funds versus direct investments. We did not set objectives for financial structures.

The final element of our philosophy was to control the investment process and not the decision. Paul Sack presented a detailed overview of any real estate investment. Sponsors are ill-suited to stay that close to it: they are poorly served by trying to second guess how the facade on a particular building should look or what the maintenance schedule should be. Real estate managers should do that. But to ensure that the individual managers you have working for you are each looking after your interest, there has to be some sense of overall maximization. In the final analysis, the amount available for pension fund real estate portfolios is the total of what the real estate managers acquire. If each manager acts independently the results will not be optimal.

Investment Vehicles Used in Developing the Real Estate Portfolio

We have used commingled funds, separately managed accounts, and company directed investments. Having also tried both open- and closed-end funds, we concur with Meyer Melnikoff's comment that in real estate what matters is the real estate itself, not the form. The commingled funds did enable both AT&T and the Bell System to go forward. Commingled funds afforded the opportunity for smaller properties. That provided an efficient way to deal with properties ranging anywhere from $2 million to $10 million, and provided a core portfolio.

The separately managed accounts, on the

other hand, gave better control over investment objectives, and helped avoid duplication. Company directed investments should also be considered by any major fund. To really get into premiere properties, you have to make a direct investment decision yourself. With $4 billion in real estate, we knew that we could not hide behind another fiduciary and say, "Well he told me it was a good idea and I just took his word." So for us, the decision to go forward and invest was not very difficult. You need to know the people you are dealing with very well; you need to be comfortable with the investment that is going to be made; and you need to get very competent legal counsel.

You also have to keep in mind the staff required. I have a staff of approximately 50 people, 25 to 30 investment professionals, 8 of whom spend almost all their time on real estate. If you plan to get into real estate deeply, you ought to take into account that it will be labor-intensive.

After all of our fundamental planning, we ended with direct investments of 61 percent at the end of the year. This is the Telephone Real Estate Equity Trust (TREET), which is the holding vehicle for the former Bell System real estate investments. Approximately 30 percent of the trust is invested in commingled funds. The remaining 9 percent is a reserve account. Since the beginning of the year, the reserve for future commitments has shrunk completely because there were commitments for a number of deals that had not yet closed at divestiture. As part of the divestiture process, we put money into the trust to fund all of those future commitments.

Factors Used in Controlling the Investment Process

When considering sponsoring a specific investment opportunity, it is important to look at size, property, location, and the financial structure offered. Generally, we actively sought the fair or unfair advantage of larger properties—if you accord size an unfair advantage—because we felt they offered better quality, better location, and better potential returns. The buyer's market is much less competitive, however. As we were assembling our portfolio, there were periods where we were literally one of two, three, or maybe four potential bidders. We could almost guarantee that we had seen every attractive large real estate deal because it was such a small market.

From an administrative standpoint, larger properties were easier to handle, so overall, it seemed, "bigger was better."

AT&T's emphasis has been on office, commercial, and industrial properties. We would like to have more industrial real estate, but it is difficult to find, particularly relative to the size of our real estate investment program. Good shopping centers at reasonable prices have also been hard to come by. Overall, shopping centers and industrial sites seem to be easier to control, in terms of occupancy and returns, than office properties. As buyers, we found a few good properties in the commercial category.

Our holdings are reasonably balanced geographically. Our office investments are fairly well distributed across the country; our commercial shopping centers are predominantly in the East and our industrial properties primarily in the West.

CRITERIA FOR EVALUATING MANAGERS

Probably the most critical choice a sponsor has to make is finding the managers who are actually going to make the real estate investments. Proper personnel is the sponsor's equivalent of "location, location, location." Investment real estate is a small world. Evaluate the people you are dealing with first and then look at the project, because every project brought to you is going to have a lot of appeal in the mind of the person that is selling it or looking for financing. To be sure you are getting value for your money, you must have the staff expertise to evaluate and review each offer and confidence in the people that are bringing you the properties. Know the people you are dealing with and also look at the properties just to get your own sense of what is going on out there.

When considering the possible financial structures, we do not rule anything out. Our preference is equity ownership, so all our debt participation holdings have equity kickers in some fashion. Yet, with the very astute and very different viewpoints in the real estate market, the investment form should not be dictated arbitrarily. Be willing, within reason, to consider a variety of different financial packages.

Maintain an open door and do not set too many guidelines regarding the kind of proposals to be considered because the market changes, the economic circumstances change, and each environment provides a unique opportunity to structure a deal.

Measuring Performance

One ongoing struggle is how to get consistent returns from the managers. We have 22 real estate managers and they all like to know how they are doing. We calculate the return on a different basis from how a manager calculates it, such that we can find 100 to 200 basis points difference. Some of that difference turns out to be caused by differences in approach and/or in philosophy regarding rates of return. Moreover, economic conditions change, sometimes inflation changes, markets always change—all of these conditions are beyond the manager's control. Yet, real estate can be controlled more than some other investments, so, if an investment is not working quite right, often the manager can make improvements that will move the process in the right direction.

A long-term perspective is necessary in assessing real estate, particularly when dealing with boards or board committees. You cannot invest 10 percent of your fund in real estate and promise a board of directors a report in 10 years. Yet, boards need to appreciate the fact that quarter-to-quarter reports do not mean anything and that year-to-year reports are questionable too. Managers likewise should be assessed, not on a year-to-year basis, but over a period of years and on how well they deliver on what they have promised.

Other Issues of Concern

Sponsors need to be concerned about ERISA, ongoing tax legislation, and issues of that nature that complicate and change the overall environment. The process is complicated, expensive, and time consuming. Initially, we were faced with a lot of difficulties with prohibited transactions. For instance, if we wanted to buy a shopping center that had a phone store in it, that was a problem. We have worked to get exemptions through the Department of Labor that take into account the nature of our business, staff expertise, and the size of our real estate portfolio. They have given us more latitude recently.

FUTURE OF REAL ESTATE IN AT&T'S FUND

AT&T plans to continue new investment in real estate. There is a real advantage to being perceived as being in the market all the time. This does not mean that you take every deal offered, but the chances for getting that once-in-a-lifetime property are much better if people know you have a little cash available for the right deal. It is up to us to decide what the right deal is, but our perceived availability does stimulate the flow.

Finally, to understand the commitment that is required, you need to be professional, bring the staff resources to bear, and stick with it. You cannot time any market; certainly you cannot time real estate markets. If you make an investment, be prepared to stick with it. We were one of Meyer's early clients in PRISA at a time when a lot of people misunderstood the liquidity built into it, which Meyer never sold as a feature. Liquidity was there, cash permitting, circumstances permitting; but in the early 1980s when a few people tried to get out and time the market they found that the liquidity was not there. Do not invest in real estate expecting it to be liquid. There is liquidity if you need to sell, but it is at a very substantial price. Real estate is a long-term investment; it is ideally suited to the way pension funds ought to invest their assets. As our actuary used to say, you must have a 90 year horizon: it is a long time and money ought to be invested accordingly.

Chambers/Feldman Question and Answer Session

QUESTION: With most pension funds investing in equities, why should I invest in whole loans?

FELDMAN: I presume you mean mortgage-backed securities of one sort or another. We tend to view those as debt securities. Real estate in our scheme has some sort of equity kicker involved in it. If it's a mortgage return, I think you've got to evaluate it just as you would any other investment: what security is involved, what return can you get for it?

QUESTION: What is your view of using International Paper timberland partnership or the paper stocks as vehicles to invest in timberland?

CHAMBERS: I asked an employee of International Paper Company about the limited partnership that they have just offered. His response was that he has not purchased any of it. I have not purchased any of it either. In the offices of one of the 100 largest corporations last week the subject came up. I'm not sure any of us yet understand the partnership; more time is needed to study the complexities of it. I refer you to my comments earlier that in relation to timberland the corporate philosophy is not to maximize return on the timber investment. Forest products companies are manufacturers mostly and if you track the performance of the forest industry, it has not been that good. So we do not feel that forest industry stock is a substitute for real estate investment or timberland investments. We think that by owning and growing the raw material, which forest industries need in order to exist, we can substantially beat their performance, the performance of Standard & Poor's, and inflation.

QUESTION: Would you comment on the tax shelter aspects of timberland investment and the likely impact of changes in the tax law proposed by the Treasury on timberland investment. Do those concern you?

CHAMBERS: Our fund is a tax exempt fund because it is for qualified employee benefit funds. We have a private letter ruling from the Internal Revenue Service that says that income from timber harvest is exempt from unrelated business taxable income. We are the only fund in the nation to have a private letter ruling of this type. We do not consider timberland as a tax shelter even for tax paying entities. There are tax advantages to timberland in that you can take depletion on the timber, which means you simply recover the cost that you put into the timber. The returns from the harvest, if they're done properly, are taxed at capital gains rate. From a timberland investment scenario, the tax changes will not affect the performance of our portfolio since we're tax free. It will allow us to compete more effectively with taxpayers for the resource. Additionally, the benefit of taxes does not create a major advantage, so even the tax paying entities will not be greatly penalized. The real losers, again, will be the forest products industry because they have so much money invested in land and timber, and capital gains tax treatment is so important to their returns.

FELDMAN: If the question referred to timberland, I agree. If it referred to real estate in general, I think for pension funds and the kinds of real estate they buy, it may in fact be a wash to a net plus over time because you will return to more of an economic value. Attractive deals were harder to find, but they were still there. I think most of the speculation and tax activities centered around investments that weren't major elements for us. We'll just have to wait and see what they come up with.

QUESTION: After ten years of experience what would you have done differently?

FELDMAN: I would have put more in sooner.

Appendix

The Role of Real Estate in a Multi-Asset Portfolio

Jeffrey J. Diermeier, CFA, J. Kurt Freundlich, and Gary G. Schlarbaum, CFA

I. INTRODUCTION

The appropriate focus of portfolio management is the total portfolio. The overall portfolio selection problem can be broken down into four separate decision problems:

1 What asset classes should be included in the portfolio?
2 What normal, or policy, weights should be assigned to the included asset classes?
3 What strategic weights should be assigned to the asset classes as a result of short-term investment insights?
4 What specific investments should be selected within the generic asset classes?

The first two decisions are policy decisions. For large, institutional portfolios, overall portfolio performance is most affected by these decisions. In fact, research indicates that 90 to 95 percent of the variation in total pension plan performance is explained by these decisions.[1] These key policy decisions are deserving of a substantial amount of time and attention.

The purpose of this paper is to address the two policy decisions from the point of view of a U.S. pension fund focusing on the possibility of making direct equity investments in real estate located in the United States.[2] The next section of the paper sets forth suitability criteria that can be used to determine what asset classes are suitable for investment by pension plans and applies the criteria to equity real estate as an asset class. It is not surprising to find that equity real estate passes muster as an asset class for pension fund portfolios.[3]

Section III then focuses on the question of the policy weight to assign equity real estate in a pension fund portfolio. Three separate approaches to the question suggest that a normal weighting of approximately 15 percent is appropriate. This weight is considerably higher than the present weight of real estate in the aggregate pension fund portfolio. But, survey data indicate that pension plan investment officers intend to increase the weighting of equity real estate in their portfolios. The most recent annual survey by Money Market Directories, Inc., finds that 8 percent of plan assets are intended to be invested in equity real estate by 1995.[4]

The final section of the paper examines the impact of real estate on the risk and return characteristics of a pension fund portfolio. The analysis therein concludes that real estate and other nontraditional investments are valuable additions to a fund portfolio.

The two policy questions considered here have been addressed in previous papers as well. In fact, there is by now a burgeoning literature on the role of real estate in pension plan portfolios.[5] The contributions of the present paper are the systematic analysis of the desirability of real estate investment using a well-defined set of suitability criteria and the determination of the normal weight in the context of a fully-diversified, multiasset portfolio containing nine separate asset classes.

---

[3] It would indeed be a banal project to discuss whether pension funds should invest in real estate; they have done so, with the first mortgage purchased by the American Express pension fund in the late 1800s. Moreover, a survey of corporate pension plans by Ellis, 1981, pp. 56–66, indicated that 22 percent of the 1,800 largest plans had equity real estate investments, either directly or through commingled funds. On the other hand, the same survey estimated that only 1.6 percent of pension fund assets were invested in real estate in 1981.

[4] See Money Market Directories, Inc., 1985.

[5] See, for example, Cullen and Blake, 1980; Downs, 1982; Ellis, 1981; Fischer, 1983; and Fogler, 1984.

---

[1] This result is reported in Brinson, Beebower, and Hood, 1984.

[2] Real estate includes domestically located office buildings, retail centers, industrial buildings, hotels, farmland, and residential dwellings not already owned by corporations, whose stock and debt are found in investor portfolios.

II. SUITABILITY CRITERIA

A systematic treatment of the question of what asset classes should be included in the pension fund portfolio requires a set of criteria which can be used to distinguish the worthy and unworthy asset classes. This set of criteria should be universally applied to all candidates for admission to the portfolio. Candidates that can be reviewed include foreign securities, commodities, consumer durables, art, private placements, and venture capital—anything that can serve as a store of value.

The goal of the screening process is to select asset classes which the investor could buy and hold and still obtain satisfactory results. The selected asset classes are those that would be held in the portfolio in the absence of special circumstances. Special circumstances could create environments whereby it might be wise to hold just about any asset for a short period of time. Most of these special circumstances would involve some superior insight on the part of the investor. We do not intend to get caught up in the special circumstances here.

The criteria are:

- Analytical
  adequate control and regulation
  marketability and liquidity
  meaningful impact
  nonredundant
  manageable estimation risk
  earning after cost investments
- Legal
- Talent availability

These represent a reasonably comprehensive list by which to test the suitability of any asset class for normal investment purposes. Unfortunately, there are no hard boundaries to the criteria for the purposes of this paper, just as there are no hard boundaries defining the elusive "prudent man." Fortunately, individual pension fund investors can be left to determine boundaries that fit with their unique situations.

The criteria are broken into three main categories: analytical, legal, and talent. With regard to most conventional forms of real estate, the latter two categories—legal and talent availability—in and of themselves do not prohibit the use of equity real estate by pension funds.

It is legal for ERISA-regulated funds to invest in equity real estate. In fact, at least one writer has suggested that the ERISA mandate for diversification may ultimately be interpreted as requiring diversification into real estate.[6] Unlike securitized assets, the right to own real estate and the property rights of the owner are determined primarily by laws of the state in which the property is located. The law affecting real estate is not entirely uniform from state to state. There is no jurisdiction within which domestic pension funds are prohibited from ownership of real estate in general, but nearly half of the states do restrict ownership of agricultural land.[7]

Prior to the Miscellaneous Revenue Act of 1980, financial leveraging of the equity position in real estate by otherwise tax-exempt employee benefit plans exposed the related portion of the property income to potential liability as Unrelated Business Taxable Income ("UBTI"). In practice, however, even before that 1980 Act, the pension investor who opted to use mortgage financing was entitled to take certain deductions against that income, including depreciation proportionate to the extent of borrowed capital involved. In many cases, those deductions would have been sufficient in the early years of ownership to eliminate any UBTI liability. The foregoing Act amended the Internal Revenue Code to remove even the potential of UBTI generally as to third-party (nonseller) financing employed by qualified pension and profit-sharing plans.

In terms of talent availability, the tremendous surge in syndication and institutional ownership of real estate since the mid-1970s has placed considerable pressure on the available pool of experienced people in the appropriate disciplines. The skills needed to address the investment management challenge of this asset class are not encompassed by any one academic degree, professional designation, or licensing requirement; they are highly fragmented. As a profession in the United States, real estate took its first steps toward an organized body of knowledge and establishment of technical credentials in the Great Depression of the 1930s. With the unprecedented level of mortgage foreclosures and workout problems that institutional lenders confronted in that period, training and meaningful credentials in appraisal and property management became a recognized need.

---

[6] Sack, 1980, p. 346.

[7] See, for example, the discussion in Thompson, 1985, p. 126.

TABLE 1. U.S. equity real estate: outstandings

	12/31/82 Outstandings (billions)					
	Investable real estate		Investable real estate including farm		Investable real estate including farm and residential	
A. Nonresidential, noncorporate, nonfarm:						
1. Structures[1]	606.9		606.9		606.9	
Less farm[2]	90.2		90.2		90.2	
		516.7		516.7		516.7
2. Land at market value[3]		798.0		798.0		798.0
3. Less mortgages:						
Book value[4]	232.6		232.6		232.6	
Average price[5]	87.11%		87.11%		87.11%	
@ Market value		202.6		202.6		202.6
Total nonres., noncorp., nonfarm		1112.2		1112.1		1112.1
B. Farm:						
1. Structures[2]				90.2		90.2
2. Land at market value[6]				770.0		770.0
3. Less mortgages:						
Book value[7]			106.7		106.7	
Average price[5]			87.11%		87.11%	
@ Market value				92.9		92.9
Total farm				767.3		767.3
C. Residential:						
1. Structures:						
Total residential less tenant occupied					1976.3	
Multifamily—10 or more units:						
Tenant-occupied res.[8]	586.1		586.1		586.1	
Multifamily inv. fraction[9]	27.71%		27.71%			
Total[10]		162.4		162.4		2582.4
2. Land[11]		NA		NA		1115.7
3. Less mortgages:						
Book value:						
Single family[12]					1096.9	
Multifamily—10 or more units:						
Multifamily[13]	148.7		148.7		148.7	
Multifamily inv. fraction[9]	27.71%		27.71%			
Total	41.2		41.2		1245.6	
Average price[5]	87.11%		87.11%		87.11%	
@ Market value		35.9		35.9		1085.0
Total residential		126.5		126.6		2593.1
Total		$1238.6		$2005.9		$4472.5

[1] John Musgrave, *Survey of Current Business,* August 1984, "Fixed Reproducible Tangible Wealth in the United States 1980–83"; current dollar net stock of fixed nonresidential private structures in noncorporate form.

[2] John Musgrave, *Survey of Current Business,* August 1984, "Fixed Reproducible Tangible Wealth in the United States 1980–83"; farm structures.

[3] Board of Governors of the Federal Reserve System, "Balance Sheets for the U.S. Economy, 1945–83"; land for nonfarm, noncorporate business.

TABLE 1. *(concluded)*

[4] Board of Governors of the Federal Reserve System, "Flow of Funds Accounts, Assets and Liabilities Outstanding 1960–83"; nonfarm, noncorporate business commercial mortgages.

[5] Average mortgage price was adapted from unpublished data supplied by Salomon Brothers on the performance and characteristics of nonconventional mortgage markets.

[6] Data on farmland values are supplied by the U.S. Department of Agriculture, *United States: Selected Statistics on Farm Real Estate, 1950–82,* unpublished.

[7] Board of Governors of the Federal Reserve System, "Flow of Funds Accounts, Assets and Liabilities Outstanding 1960–83"; farm mortgages.

[8] John Musgrave, *Survey of Current Business,* August 1984, "Fixed Reproducible Tangible Wealth in the United States 1980–83"; current dollar net stock of residential capital in tenant occupied form.

[9] Data derived from U.S. Department of Commerce, U.S. Bureau of the Census *Current Housing Reports,* Series H-150–81, *General Housing Characteristics for the United States and Regions: 1981,* Annual Housing Survey: 1981, Part A. Fraction is the ratio of all renter-occupied housing with ten or more units in a structure as a percent of all renter-occupied year-round housing units.

[10] John Musgrave, *Survey of Current Business,* August 1984, "Fixed Reproducible Tangible Wealth in the United States 1980–83"; current dollar net stock of residential capital nonfarm owner and tenant occupied less corporate and government nonfarm.

[11] Board of Governors of the Federal Reserve System, "Balance Sheets for the U.S. Economy, 1945–83"; owner occupied and nonprofit institution land.

[12] Board of Governors of the Federal Reserve System, "Flow of Funds Accounts, Assets and Liabilities Outstanding 1960–83"; household mortgages.

[13] Board of Governors of the Federal Reserve System, "Flow of Funds Accounts, Assets and Liabilities Outstanding 1960–83"; non-U.S. government, multifamily residential mortgages.

Note: NA = not available.

Source: First Chicago Investment Advisors.

Today there are several appraisal societies of national scope, at least two major property management organizations, and another dozen professional associations that award credentials credibly linked to experience and training in various facets of acquiring, divesting, and managing income properties. There are a significant number of universities that have separate departments for real estate and urban land economics, and an even larger number that offer majors in real estate, usually through their colleges of business. There is really no question that a body of knowledge has been formalized and a systematic approach exists for its promulgation through academia and professional societies sufficient to assure that the necessary talent can be brought to bear on real estate as an investable asset class. There may be a question of the cost to acquire the necessary talent to manage a portfolio being greater than its benefit, but that should be evaluated through analytical criteria.

The first of the analytical criteria is adequate control and regulation. The existence of property, liability, and title insurance; education, ethics, and disciplinary bodies within the major professional societies; a relatively settled body of statutory and case law defining ownership rights, albeit with slight variations among the states; and a long track record of pension fund involvement in the real estate market certainly suggest that the necessary controls exist.

The second analytical criterion involves marketability and liquidity. A free and open marketplace does not guarantee a pension investor the opportunity to convert asset class holdings to another form at the time required. The market needs sufficient depth, breadth, and convertability to be able to handle the size of transactions that large pension funds need to accomplish. Note that daily liquidity may not be a necessary requirement; rather, sufficient liquidity could be provided by some combination of being able to plan cash flows and principal conversion and the ability to sell an asset in a reasonably short time span, even if at a loss.

Although real estate is believed to be fairly illiquid, the presence of other liquid assets in the typical pension portfolio does not require that real estate be particularly liquid. Furthermore, the steady cash throw-off of this generally high-yield asset class, combined with sale capabilities suggest that, in the broad scope, the asset class is reasonably convertible. For most commercial real estate, ready buyers stand willing and able to relieve the investor of his holdings at a price.

Meaningful impact is the third analytical criterion. Simply stated, if the total value of an asset class were insufficient to allow a material holding in the portfolios of the $1.3 trillion pension fund industry, it could be rejected. Assuming a material position is one of 3 to 5 percent, this requires an asset class value of approximately $39 to $65 billion in assets. The real estate industry, even after removing single-family residences, farm

TABLE 2.   U.S. equity real estate: proportions

		12/31/82 Proportions		
		Investable real estate	*Investable real estate including farm*	*Investable real estate including farm and residential*
A.	**Nonresidential, noncorporate, nonfarm:**			
	Structures	41.7%	25.8%	11.6%
	Land	64.4	39.8	17.8
	Mortgages	16.4	10.1	4.5
	Total	89.8	55.4	24.9
B.	**Farm:**			
	Structures		4.5	2.0
	Land		38.4	17.2
	Mortgages		4.6	2.1
	Total		38.3	17.2
C.	**Residential:**			
	Structures	13.1	8.1	57.3
	Land	NA	NA	24.9
	Mortgages	2.9	1.8	24.3
	Total	10.2	6.3	58.0
	Total	100.0%	100.0%	100.0%

Source: First Chicago Investment Advisors.

properties, and corporate held real estate, easily surpasses that hurdle.

We are interested in the equity only portion of this noncorporate real estate, as the investment economics of mortgages on real estate can be obtained by the plan sponsor by other means.[8] Mortgage pass-through securities amounted to approximately $155 billion at market value at year-end 1982. These could, of course, be put under the real estate label, depending upon the user of the data.

Table 1 gives three alternative measures of the size of noncorporate, equity real estate at market values as of 12/31/82. The first definition focuses primarily on nonresidential, nonfarm, noncorporate structures, and the land underneath them less mortgages. Pension fund holdings of office buildings, shopping centers, hotels, and industrial space would fall under this category, as would holdings by partnerships and pro-

prietorships.[9] A minor slice of the residential market is included to take into consideration the availability of ownership of larger apartment dwellings by plan sponsors. This set of definitions leads to the conclusion that as of year-end 1982, $1.24 trillion of equity real estate was in existence.

The second alternative definition folds in farmland and farm structures less mortgages. Work by Kaplan suggests this little-used asset type is very appropriate for pension plan investment, particularly because of the nondepreciable nature of land investment for tax purposes.[10] However, the local statutes restricting ownership and the unpredictability of federal government policies affecting farm operations have made pension funds reluctant to move into this asset type. This definition provides a year-end 1982 market value to equity real estate of $2.01 trillion.

The final alternative definition adds to the collection all residential structures and land less mortgages. In so doing, the real estate pie swells

[8] First, the sponsor can buy the stocks of banks, savings and loans, and insurance companies, and thereby lay indirect claim to a large amount of the real estate debt market. Secondly, he can buy mortgage pass-through securities, which provide for direct real estate debt investment. We capture this pass-through debt under the asset class label of U.S. fixed-income securities.

[9] A separate estimate of foundation investment holdings is not included because of discontinuities in historic data, but is estimated to amount to just over $1 billion.

[10] See Kaplan.

to $4.47 trillion. We have generally not used this broad definition of real estate for two reasons. First, there is not presently a direct profitable vehicle to purchase single family residences for pension funds on any scale. Secondly, as our primary focus is on the pension investable capital market, we do not want to confuse investment with current consumption. Similarly, if we were measuring pension investable cash equivalents, we would not include transaction-balance money supply assets, because of their role as a facilitator of consumption as opposed to a role as a store of wealth. Both examples raise tough empirical issues of substitutability of consumption for investment and the splitting out of the two components where they exist in the same asset.

The composition of the real estate market under those three definitions is shown in Table 2 and Figure 1.

The fourth analytical criterion is nonredundancy. The issue is whether an asset class simply duplicates return opportunities that are available elsewhere or represents an additional set of opportunities. An asset class should not be included in a pension fund policy portfolio unless it regularly provides additional return opportunities or provides opportunities in a more desirable form than existing asset classes.

FIGURE 1
Investable real estate—12/31/82

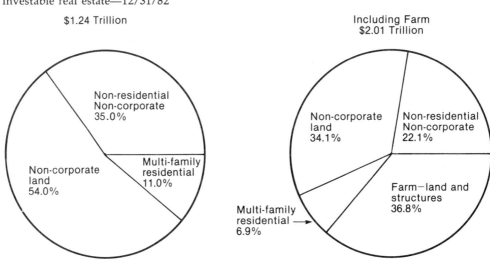

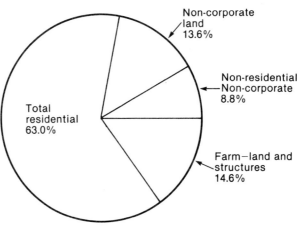

Source: First Chicago Investment Advisors.

Historically, pension funds have held only domestic stocks, bonds, and cash in their portfolios. One might argue that these funds should invest in real estate through the stock market if there were enough stocks that are essentially "real estate" stocks. The real estate trusts provide examples of real estate stocks. Companies such as Georgia Pacific and Weyerhaeuser do so as well. And, it is true that many of the common stocks held by pension funds provide real estate returns as part of an overall package of returns.

Unfortunately, a strong and efficient real estate investment trust industry has not evolved. Moreover, there are significant portions of the real estate market that can be acquired, in sufficient amounts, only through direct equity real estate investments.[11] Clearly, real estate should not be excluded because it is a redundant asset class.

The fifth analytical criterion involves estimation risk. Bawa, Brown and Klein have shown that estimation risk can be a sufficient condition for not owning a valued asset.[12]

The issue regarding real estate is whether or not the pension investor can make forecasts of expected returns, of the variation of returns, and of the covariance of real estate returns with the returns from other investments that are sufficiently reliable for making investment judgments. Real estate returns are more difficult to measure than the returns provided by marketable securities. This is because parcels of real estate change hands infrequently. As a result, rates of return cannot be determined on the basis of observed transactions; they must be estimated on the basis of appraisals. Nonetheless, it is possible to draw reasonable inferences about expected return, about the likelihood of loss if one wanted to liquidate at an inopportune time, and about its relation to other asset classes. Real estate should not be excluded on the basis of estimation risk. On the contrary, many real estate professionals believe that the returns on real estate assets are much more estimable than those of common stocks.

The final analytical criterion we call earning after cost investments. This designation is controversial; a strict aggregate portfolio view could be taken and the criterion labeled "sufficient portfolio value added." With that change, even economically wasting assets with negative expected real returns could be included as a buy and hold portfolio asset if the asset contained sufficient portfolio risk-reduction properties.[13]

An ample history and body of evidence exist to suggest that after all costs, real estate has, as an asset class, thrown off positive real rates of return.

A review of the three categories of suitability criteria—analytical, legal, talent—strongly suggests that real estate qualifies as being a legitimate portfolio holding. The next logical question is, at what normal level does it qualify, given the competing alternatives?

III. THE NORMAL REAL ESTATE WEIGHTING

The second policy decision involves the assignment of investment policy weights to the asset classes included in the portfolio. The policy, or normal, weight assigned to an asset class is the weight assigned in the absence of any specific insights about relative asset class performance. It represents the appropriate default or neutral portfolio proportion after systematic equilibrium conditions have been estimated.

The focus of this section is the appropriate normal weight for real estate in the portfolio of a typical pension plan. Three separate approaches for determining the normal weight are developed. The first approach, based on the capital asset pricing model, determines the proportion of the entire investable capital market made up of real estate. The second uses the New Equilibrium Theory of Ibbotson, Diermeier, and Siegel, which relaxes some of the restrictive assumptions of the capital asset pricing model and also incorporates nonrisk variables, to suggest appropriate shadings of market value weights.[14] The third approach is more quantitative, but probably not any more precise. It uses the mean-variance optimization framework of Markowitz to determine an appropriate normal weighting for real estate.[15]

[13] An obvious example of such an asset is gold. Gold is excluded under our criteria. If the "sufficient portfolio value added" criteria were adopted, the issue would be whether gold is sufficiently negatively correlated with other primary asset classes. In general, gold has a spotty record of performance as an insurance asset. It is only at times of great universal calamity that gold has performed its insurance role well.

[14] Ibbotson, Diermeier, and Siegel, 1984, pp. 74–80 and pp. 22–33.

[15] Markowitz, 1952, pp. 77–91, and 1959.

[11] An example is the commercial office sector.
[12] See Bawa, Brown, and Klein, 1979.

Market Value Approach

A logical starting point in the determination of the normal weighting of real estate in a plan sponsor portfolio is the proportion of the total market portfolio made up of real estate. A naive reading of extant capital market theory suggests that every investor should hold, appropriately leveraged, the "market portfolio" which, by definition, includes all risky assets in proportion to their outstanding market values. The assumptions underlying the development of the capital asset pricing model lead to this prescription. And, even more sophisticated approaches to the portfolio selection problem which recognize different investor tax situations, constraints, and so on, suggest the market portfolio as a logical starting point. For example, the following quote from Bill Sharpe illustrates our point:

> One should hardly conclude that every investor should hold a market-value balanced portfolio. Cash requirements, tax situations, legal and institutional restrictions, investment horizons and predictions differ. But divergences from the standard mix of bonds and stocks should be justifiable in terms of these differences.[16]

First Chicago Investment Advisors has expended considerable effort to determine the relative proportions of the pension investable asset classes as well as the aggregate market value of the asset classes.[17] As shown in Figure 2, our work indicates that equity real estate represents 14 to 37 percent of the aggregate market value of the pension investable asset classes. When farmland and residential real estate are excluded from the universe, real estate comprises 14.0 percent of the pension investable capital markets. Adding farmland increases the real estate weighting to 20.9 percent. The further addition of residential real estate brings the total proportion in real estate to 37.0 percent.

We recognize that there is room for differing opinions on the appropriate composition of the real estate asset class. Nonetheless, it is reasonable to conclude that an argument that market

value weighting is appropriate points toward a normal weight of somewhere between 14 percent and 37 percent for real estate. Our preferred definition of the pension investable real estate market, as discussed previously, would indicate a normal weight between 14 and 21 percent.

The assumptions leading to the conclusion that all investors should hold the "market portfolio" include the assumptions that there are no taxes and transaction costs and that all investors have the same investment horizon. Obviously, none of these assumptions holds, and as a result, the differing characteristics of investors and assets will often lead to certain clienteles. Desirable weights for an asset class in a portfolio are dependent upon the characteristics of the asset class and the investor.

In the next section, the question of whether the characteristics of real estate as an asset class and pension funds as investors are such that real estate should be given a nonmarket weight is considered in the context of the New Equilibrium Theory developed by Ibbotson, Diermeier, and Siegel.[18]

NET Approach

The New Equilibrium Theory (NET) explicitly recognizes that investors are heterogeneous, having different tax situations and institutional constraints, and different time horizons. NET assumes that investors regard each asset as a bundle of characteristics, some risk oriented, some nonrisk oriented. Investors heterogeneously translate each characteristic into a cost and require compensation in the form of expected return for bearing the costs. Hence, in this framework, investors are interested in returns net of all investor costs, individually determined. These costs are theorized to include costs of all risks, taxes, and immarketability.

The question we pose here is the following: Relative to the typical investor, should plan sponsor investors own more or less real estate because of their NET characteristics? The prior section has put forth some data regarding the market value weight of real estate. We use a simple rating scheme to determine whether pension funds should tilt to more or less than a market weight.

First, a listing of the characteristics of plan

---

[16] Sharpe, 1973, pp. 74–80.

[17] This effort has been a joint undertaking with the firm of R. G. Ibbotson and Company. Published papers based on this work include Ibbotson, Carr, and Robinson, 1984; and Ibbotson and Siegel, 1984.

[18] Ibbotson, Diermeier, and Siegel, 1984.

FIGURE 2
Investable capital market—12/31/82

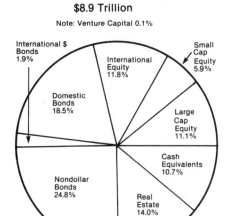

$8.9 Trillion
Note: Venture Capital 0.1%

International $ Bonds 1.9%
International Equity 11.8%
Small Cap Equity 5.9%
Domestic Bonds 18.5%
Large Cap Equity 11.1%
Cash Equivalents 10.7%
Nondollar Bonds 24.8%
Real Estate 14.0%

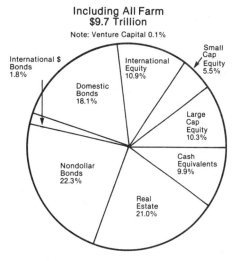

Including All Farm
$9.7 Trillion
Note: Venture Capital 0.1%

International $ Bonds 1.8%
International Equity 10.9%
Small Cap Equity 5.5%
Domestic Bonds 18.1%
Large Cap Equity 10.3%
Cash Equivalents 9.9%
Nondollar Bonds 22.3%
Real Estate 21.0%

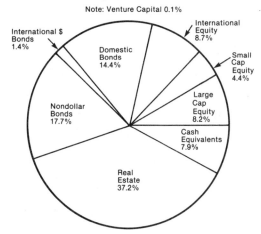

Including Farm and All Residential
$12.2 Trillion
Note: Venture Capital 0.1%

International $ Bonds 1.4%
Domestic Bonds 14.4%
International Equity 8.7%
Small Cap Equity 4.4%
Large Cap Equity 8.2%
Cash Equivalents 7.9%
Nondollar Bonds 17.7%
Real Estate 37.2%

Source: First Chicago Investment Advisors.

sponsors is necessary. Some fairly standard characterizations are:

- Large size
- Long horizon
- U.S. based domicile
- ERISA governance
- Tax-exempt status
- Total return objective

Table 3 lists security characteristics as originally discussed by Ibbotson, Diermeier, and Siegel and later expanded upon by Ibbotson and Siegel.[19] In terms of economy risk, real estate is believed to have a high sensitivity, but because of the long investment horizon of plan sponsors, this is a less negative characteristic than with the "typical" investor.

Real estate has the relatively unique characteristic of not being very vulnerable to unanticipated changes in inflation. This is a valuable characteristic for most investors. Because, however, pension funds currently make use of few inflation

[19] Ibbotson and Siegel, 1984.

TABLE 3. Characteristic scoring

Security characteristic	U.S. real estate rating	Plan sponsor relative attraction
A. Risk:		
Economy risk	High	+
Inflation risk	Low	+
Real interest rate risk	High	0
Currency risk	Zero	+
Residual risk	High	+
B. Marketability:		
Information costs	High	+
Transaction costs	High	+
Divisibility costs	High	+
C. Taxability	Variable	−

Source: First Chicago Investment Advisors.

hedging investment vehicles, and because the large component of household wealth is already held in the form of the home, investment real estate is relatively more attractive to the plan sponsor.

All investments are sensitive to real interest rates. Real estate may be thought of as being more sensitive because of its linkage to the volatile construction industry. It is not clear whether the pension or typical nonpension investor is more sensitive to this factor.

U.S. pension plans are prohibited from directly investing in foreign real estate under ERISA. As a result, the investable capital market has been described without foreign real estate, which some have estimated casually to be 40 percent of world wealth. This restriction on foreign real estate investment will tend to make domestic real estate investment more attractive than would otherwise be the case.

Residual risk arises when it is not possible to hold fully diversified portfolios. U.S. real estate's high ranking on this variable reflects the relatively high costs of diversification associated with real estate investing. The large size of pension plans suggests that it is easier for them to diversify than for the individual investor with a huge mortgage.

Marketability is often referred to as liquidity, and we use the terms interchangeably. Regarding the three marketability characteristics—information costs, transaction costs, and divisibility costs—it is fairly clear to see that the large size and the suspected longer planning horizon of the

typical plan sponsor gives material advantage over the typical investor. Economies of scale and long holding periods would tend to hold these costs down for the typical plan sponsor. It appears to be the basic rule that pension plans are better able to capture illiquidity premiums that might be imbedded in security returns by liquidity-minded investors. Furthermore, restrictions on the part of some real estate investment vehicles that prohibit immediate withdrawal of investment put a high premium on being able to forego immediate liquidity.

The final security characteristics of this NET framework approach involves taxability. It is commonly believed, because of the tax-advantaged nature of real estate, that pension plans compete for properties whose pieces carry a substantial premium established by taxable entities.[20] At issue here is whether real estate is more tax-advantaged to the taxable investor than other investment alternatives and if so, the degree to which the tax-advantaged investor might bid up prices to capture the advantage.

The impact of taxation on the pricing of securities is very complicated because of the overlapping, special interest nature of the tax code. Stepwise tax brackets, capital gains, accelerated depreciation, multiple taxing authorities, and all such, make it extremely hard to handle this issue in totality. As a result, our analysis will make some very simplifying assumptions.

Tax benefits are available to taxable investors who invest in real estate. The cost of real estate (less land) may be depreciated for tax purposes at a rate that generally far exceeds any actual declines in the value of the property. The result is both a deferral of taxes and a conversion of ordinary income to long-term capital gains. Tax credits are also a direct benefit of equity investments in real estate. Finally, the use of debt financing in the purchase of real estate leads to interest payments that are deductible for the taxable investor.[21]

It is obvious that all of the tax benefits accrue to taxable investors. As we will show, however, the tax-exempt investor earns a higher return on good real estate investments that are 100 percent financed with equity because he does not split

[20] See, for example, the discussion in Fischer, 1983.

[21] Of course, none of these advantages is unique to real estate. For example, debt financing can be used in the purchase of bonds and stocks.

TABLE 4. Comparison of unleveraged returns to taxable and tax-exempt investors*

| | (1) | (2) | (3) |
| | | After-tax return to taxable investor in the 50 percent | |
	Return to tax-exempt investor	bracket	(2) ÷ (1)
Treasury bills	7.5%	3.75%	0.500
Long-term government bonds	10.5	5.25	0.500
Large cap equities	13.5	9.3	0.689
Small cap equities	15.25	11.6	0.761
Real estate:			
Coopers-Lybrand projection†	12.9	9.9	0.767
FCIA projection††	14.1	10.8	0.766

* For the first four asset classes, rates of return to the tax-exempt investor are based on long-term required rates developed by First Chicago Investment Advisors. Assumed dividend yields are 5 percent for large cap equities and 2 percent for small cap equities. The rates of return for real estate are the result of projections for a single project in each case and assume 100 percent equity financing. In all cases, it is assumed that the before-tax investment returns are identical for the tax-exempt and taxable investor.
† Projection contained in Hansen [10].
†† Based on actual FCIA investment project undertaken in 1984.
Source: First Chicago Investment Advisors.

shares with Uncle Sam, while the taxable investor, despite all of the tax benefits, generally does.

It is possible, however, for the taxable investor to earn a higher after-tax rate of return when debt financing is used. And, an investor in the 50 percent tax bracket is unlikely to forego the benefits inherent in the use of debt financing. Projected rates of return for tax-exempt and taxable investors in both the unleveraged and leveraged situations are shown in Tables 4 and 5.

Table 4 shows unleveraged rates of return to two investors, one tax-exempt, and the other in the 50 percent marginal tax bracket.[22] Rates of return for the tax-exempt investor are shown in column 1; rates of return for the taxable investor are shown in column 2. The ratio of the after-tax rate to the before-tax rate for each asset class is listed in column 3.

The ratios in column 3 provide a useful reading on the degree of the tax advantage. The higher the ratio, the greater the degree of tax advantage. The table shows that real estate is more of a "tax-advantaged" investment than large capitalization equities, bonds, and Treasury bills. However, real estate is very similar to small capitalization equities in this regard.

In sum, real estate is the most tax advantaged of the usual pension investable asset classes, but it is very similar to low yielding equities and not

dramatically different from large capitalization equities with higher yields.

The use of debt financing increases the ratio of taxable investor returns to tax-exempt investor returns in every case. The increase is most dramatic in the case of real estate, where the ratios increase from 0.77 to greater than 1.1. The ratios of real estate are now considerably higher than the ratio for small capitalization equities. The tax advantage of real estate is greatly magnified by the use of leverage.[23] It is necessary to remember that the returns included in Tables 4 and 5 are expected returns, and leverage does work both ways. Extensive use of leverage results in greatly increased volatility of equity returns.

There are factors that work to reduce the influence of current tax advantages. First, as land is generally nondepreciable, the larger the land component, the less is the tax advantage. This has been argued as a reason why farmland is a particularly attractive asset class for pension funds.[24] According to the Federal Reserve Board Flow of Funds accounts, 30 percent of the value of all property is locked into the land beneath

[22] It is assumed that the taxable investor pays taxes at the statutory rate and does not engage in the tax avoidance techniques suggested in Miller and Scholes, 1978.

[23] The relative change in the ratios is partially a result of the fact that debt financing is used more extensively in the real estate market. Current margin requirements limit the use of leverage in the equity market. In the case of 75 percent debt financing, the ratio for small capitalization equities is 1.037. This is still less than the ratios for real estate, but not so dramatic.

[24] See Kaplan.

TABLE 5. Comparison of leveraged returns to taxable and tax-exempt investors*

	(1) Return to tax-exempt investor	(2) After-tax return to taxable investor in the 50 percent bracket	(3) (2) ÷ (1)
Large cap equities†	16.5%	13.3%	0.806
Small cap equities†	20.0	17.9	0.895
Real estate:			
Coopers-Lybrand projection††	16.3	18.6	1.141
FCIA projection§§	15.7	17.3	1.102

* The rates of return in this table are based on the rates of return shown in Table 4. In all cases, it is assumed that a portion of the purchase price of the asset is borrowed.
† It is assumed that 50 percent of the purchase price is borrowed at an interest rate of 10.5 percent.
†† Calculation assumes a 75 percent mortgage at a rate of 14 percent.
§§ Calculation assumes a 70 percent mortgage at a rate of 13.5 percent.
Source: First Chicago Investment Advisors.

it. This suggests that one-third of the property cannot participate in the depreciation advantages.

Secondly, the gyrations of the tax code itself reduce the degree to which the experienced investor makes full use of the tax code. With the major alterations to the real estate tax code in the last four years, taxable investors should take into consideration tax policy risk when assessing their desire for tax-advantaged properties. In a period of huge government deficits, the wary investor knows that less politically protected tax breaks are continuous candidates for modification or elimination.

Overall we conclude from the foregoing that strong arguments exist for both higher and lower than normal real estate positions on the part of pension funds. On balance, the arguments presented here lead us to the conclusion that there is no apparent rationale for a dramatic departure from market weighting of real estate in the pension plan portfolio. On the basis of the capital market definition which includes farmland but excludes single family residential, a weighting of 15 percent to 20 percent appears justified.

Markowitz Approach

A third approach that can be used to obtain the appropriate normal weighting for real estate is portfolio optimization. We have used this approach to develop the Multiple Markets Index (MMI), a comprehensive index used as the benchmark for measuring the performance of our Multi-Asset Portfolio (MAP) Fund. Real estate is one of the nine asset classes included in the MMI, and the weight assigned to it is 15 percent.

The complete composition of the MMI is shown in Figure 3.[25]

The optimization process which produced the MMI used the inputs shown in Tables 6 and 7. The only constraints placed on the optimizations were that all weights must be nonnegative and the maximum weight for venture capital is 5 percent. The mean-variance efficient portfolio with estimated risk equal to that of the typical pension fund was selected as the MMI.[26] The complete process of developing the MMI is set forth in Brinson, Diermeier, and Schlarbaum.[27] Our purpose here is to describe, briefly, the development of the necessary inputs for the real estate asset class.

The estimates used in the optimization process are long-term estimates. They are developed in a framework where expected return is positively and systematically related to risk. As a result, the initial step in obtaining the needed inputs is to develop estimates of variances and covariances for each of the asset classes.

The starting point for our estimate of the standard deviation of returns for each asset class is the historical record of returns from that asset class. Twenty-four month rolling standard deviations are determined for each month for which information is available. The historical record of the rolling standard deviations and our interpre-

[25] Only eight asset classes are shown in the figure. The ninth asset class is cash, which is assigned a normal weight of zero percent.
[26] The risk of the MMI is essentially the same as the risk of a portfolio containing 60 percent domestic equities and 40 percent domestic bonds.
[27] See Brinson, Diermeier, and Schlarbaum, 1985.

FIGURE 3
Multiple Markets Index

Components

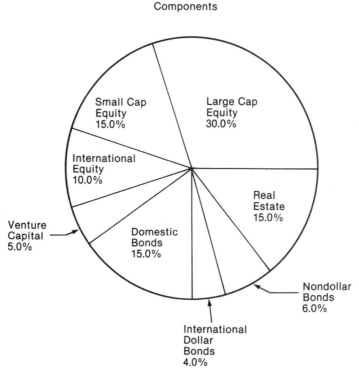

Source: First Chicago Investment Advisors.

tations of the causes and persistence of that record provide the basis for our estimate. The resulting estimate allows for any trends in volatility that have occurred in the recent past.

Real estate presents some special problems in this framework. Publicly available real estate return series have lacked credibility because the return patterns appear too smooth.[28] Compared with stocks and bonds, real estate properties are traded very infrequently. As a result, it is necessary to rely on appraisals to obtain "market values" rather than observing transactions. Observers more familiar with securities markets are concerned that an appraisal value does not define the price required to clear the market at an instant in time. In fact, the appraiser's definition of "market value" allows a "reasonable time for exposure in the open market." Appraisal methodology necessarily tends to rely more on lagged than on immediate perceptions of the market.

[28] An exception is the series developed by Hoag, 1980. The "FRC Property Index" published by NCREIF may turn out to be an exception as well. However, the latter series covers too short a time period since its inception at the end of 1977 to provide conclusive evidence.

Participants in the real estate market argue that the current appraisal methodology reflects the way that business is done. As a result, they contend it is not fair to criticize appraisal values. Nonetheless, there is a problem of comparing a measure of risk developed using existing real estate return series and one obtained using return series for stocks and bonds. For our purposes, it was necessary to develop a more comparable series of real estate returns in order to estimate the standard deviation of returns from real estate.

The returns earned by equity real estate investment trusts (REITs) are the building blocks for our real estate return series. On a monthly basis, an unweighted average of the returns of the available equity REITs was determined. The historical record of this series provides the basis for our estimate of the standard deviation of real estate returns.

The estimation of standard deviation based on the REIT series is supplemented by an estimation of the duration of the properties held in First Chicago Investment Advisors' real estate Fund F. This analysis indicates an average duration of approximately 9.5 years, based on projected cash

TABLE 6. Optimization inputs

	Risk premium	Less passive fee	Realizable risk premium*	Risk*
Large cap	5.80%	.10	5.70%	16.50%
Small cap	7.55	.20	7.35	22.00
International equity	6.35	.25	6.10	20.50
Venture capital	15.00	2.00	13.00	40.00
Domestic bonds	2.30	.10	2.20	8.50
Dollar bonds	2.25	.10	2.15	8.00
Non-dollar bonds	2.70	.15	2.55	12.00
Real estate	4.80	.80	4.00	14.00
T bills	0.00	.00	.00	1.50

* Optimization inputs.
Source: First Chicago Investment Advisors.

flows. This is longer than the duration of a 20-year government bond at this point in time. The average is consistent with a standard deviation for real estate that is greater than that for long government bonds.[29]

The estimation of the necessary correlation coefficients is based on two key inputs. The first is the historical record of 24-month rolling correlation coefficients. Again, REIT data were used as a proxy for real estate returns. The second key input is a set of survey results obtained by asking internal asset class specialists about the relationship between the returns on their asset class and numerous fundamental and political variables. Their responses were then used to infer the correlation structure.

Notice that the correlation coefficients in Ta-

ble 7 involving real estate are considerably higher than those reported elsewhere in the literature. A table containing correlation coefficients between real estate and stocks and bonds drawn from a number of different studies is included in the recent paper by Zerbst and Cambon.[30] All of the correlation coefficients relating stock returns and real estate returns are negative. Our estimate of the correlation between real estate and large capitalization equities is 0.5. Our view is that the previous estimates rely too much upon the problematic historical returns and are not as reliable as ours, which are heavily influenced by the survey results.

In sum, the use of portfolio optimization requires particular care in developing the necessary inputs for the real estate asset class. The available historical data are less reliable than the historical data for stocks and bonds. There is more room for differences of opinion and controversy.

[29] A legal analysis of current bankruptcy law as it pertains to landlords of defaulting lessees indicates that the risk of loss in this situation is considerable. The bankruptcy laws favor the defaulting lessee. This again suggests more risk in real estate than in government bonds.

[30] Zerbst and Cambon, 1984, pp. 5–20.

TABLE 7. Long-term asset class correlation forecasts

	1	2	3	4	5	6	7	8	9
1. Domestic large capitalization equities	1.00								
2. Domestic small capitalization equities	.85	1.00							
3. International equities	.55	.55	1.00						
4. Venture capital	.40	.45	.55	1.00					
5. Domestic fixed income	.45	.40	.30	.15	1.00				
6. International dollar fixed income	.45	.40	.35	.20	.90	1.00			
7. Non-dollar fixed income	.15	.25	.70	.40	.40	.40	1.00		
8. Real estate	.50	.55	.50	.45	.30	.35	.30	1.00	
9. Cash equivalents	.00	.00	.00	.00	.00	.00	.00	.00	1.00

Source: First Chicago Investment Advisors.

The inputs developed at First Chicago Investment Advisors and used in the optimization process which produced the MMI indicate a policy weight for real estate of 15 percent. In fact, all three of the approaches used to determine the normal weighting of real estate in a pension fund portfolio have led to essentially the same result. Assuming that single family residences should not be included in pension fund investable real estate, the appropriate policy weight is in the range of 15 to 20 percent.

IV. THE IMPACT OF REAL ESTATE ON PORTFOLIO PERFORMANCE

We have concluded that real estate is a desirable asset class for a pension fund and that an appropriate normal weighting for real estate is approximately 15 to 20 percent. The crucial consideration is the impact of real estate on the risk and return characteristics of a pension fund portfolio. This issue is the focus of this concluding section.

The impact of adding an additional asset class to an existing portfolio is dependent upon the composition of the existing portfolio. The impact of adding an additional asset class when the existing portfolio contains only one or two is great. The marginal impact of adding an additional asset class when the current portfolio already includes seven or eight asset classes is not as great.

Two separate analyses were performed to determine the impact of real estate on the risk and return characteristics of a pension plan portfolio. In the first case, efficient frontiers were generated for the full set of asset classes included in the Multiple Markets Index and for all of these asset classes except real estate. The resulting efficient frontiers are shown in Figure 4.

The two efficient sets shown in Figure 4 lie very close to one another and are difficult to distinguish. In fact, the addition of real estate adds only five or six basis points to the expected return for lower risk portfolios and fewer than that at the high risk end of the efficient frontiers. A hasty conclusion, based on this result, is that the presence or absence of real estate as an investment class is a virtual nonevent from a performance perspective.

FIGURE 4
Attainable efficient frontiers

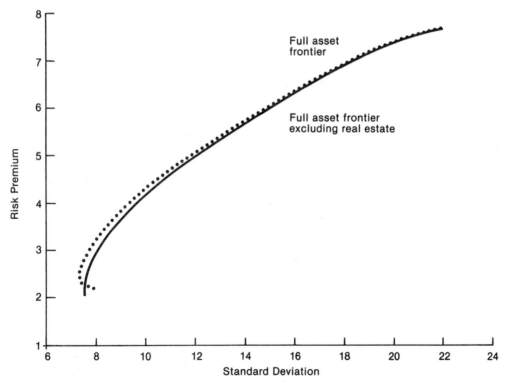

Source: First Chicago Investment Advisors.

FIGURE 5
Attainable efficient frontiers

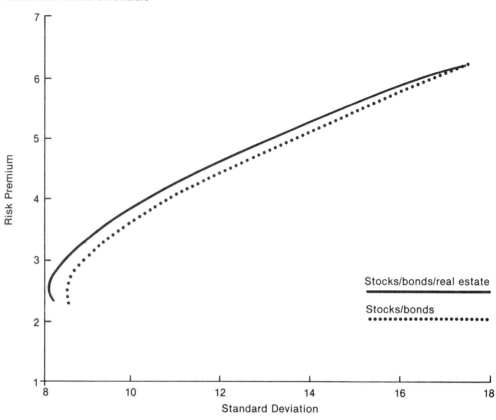

Risk Premium

Standard Deviation

Stocks/bonds/real estate

Stocks/bonds

Source: First Chicago Investment Advisors.

But, as indicated above, treating an asset class as the last addition to a portfolio is a particularly strenuous test of the contribution of that asset class to performance. The addition of all of the nontraditional asset classes included in the Multiple Markets Index to the stock/bond opportunity set provides a highly significant increase of roughly 60 basis points in expected return when risk is held constant at the level of the typical pension plan.[31] However, the 60 basis points is spread over all of the traditional asset classes. Viewed in this light, the 5 or 6 basis points is not so small.

We treated real estate as the first addition to the traditional asset classes in our second analysis of the impact of real estate. Figure 5 shows efficient frontiers for stocks and bonds only, and for stocks, bonds, and real estate. The effect of

[31] The 60 basis points is net of what we consider passive fees. These are the fees that would be incurred necessarily if a pension fund were to participate in an asset class at the most passive level of management.

adding real estate is more dramatic in this case. It provides an additional 25 basis points at the risk level of the typical pension fund.

We also examined the impact of several of our other nontraditional asset classes on the efficient frontier when each was treated as the first addition to the stock/bond opportunity set. The increases in expected return were quite comparable to those obtained when real estate was added. For example, the addition of international equities alone provided less of an increment in expected return at the low risk end of the efficient frontier and more of an increment at the high end.

The essential point is not that one of these nontraditional asset classes is more important than the others. All of them are useful and enhance the performance of a pension plan portfolio. All of them should be included. Real estate, while not unique in this regard, is certainly a valuable asset class in a multiasset pension plan portfolio.

BIBLIOGRAPHY

Bawa, V.; S. Brown; and R. Klein. *Estimating Risk and Optimal Portfolio Choice.* Amsterdam: North-Holland, 1979.

Brinson, G.; G. Beebower; and L. R. Hood. "The Determinants of Portfolio Volatility." Mimeographed. Chicago: First Chicago Investment Advisors, 1984.

Brinson, G. P.; J. J. Diermeier; and G. G. Schlarbaum. "A Composite Portfolio Performance Benchmark for Pension Plan Sponsors." Mimeographed. Chicago: First Chicago Investment Advisors, February 1985.

Cullen, T. F.; and B. Blake. "How Does Real Estate as an Investment Compare With Stocks and Bonds?" *Trusts & Estates* 119. July 1980.

Downs, A. "Should Pension Funds Own Real Estate Equities?" *National Real Estate Investor* October 1982.

Ellis, C. D. "On Pension Funds and Real Estate." *Pension World* 17. September 1981.

Fischer, J. D. "Portfolio Construction: Real Estate." In *Managing Investment Portfolios.* Eds. J. L. Maginn and D. L. Tuttle. New York: Warren, Gorham & Lamont, Inc., 1983.

Fogler, H. R. "20% in Real Estate: Can Theory Justify It?" *The Journal of Portfolio Management* 10. Winter 1984.

Fogler, H. R.; M. R. Granito; and L. R. Smith. "A Theoretical Analysis of Real Estate Returns." Mimeographed. December 1984.

Hanson, R. A. "Real Estate Investment Returns of Taxable and Non-Taxable Investors." Chicago: Coopers & Lybrand, April 1982.

Hoag, J. W. "Towards Indices of Real Estate Value and Return." *The Journal of Finance* 35. May 1980.

Ibbotson, R. G.; R. C. Carr; and A. W. Robinson. "International Equity and Bond Returns." *Financial Analysts Journal* 38. July/August 1984.

Ibbotson, R. G.; J. J. Diermeier; and L. B. Siegel. "The Demand for Capital Market Returns." *Financial Analysts Journal* 40. March/April 1984.

————. "The Demand for Capital Market Returns: A New Equilibrium Theory." *Financial Analysts Journal* 40. January/February 1984.

Ibbotson, R. G.; and L. B. Siegel. "Real Estate Returns: A Comparison With Other Investments." *AREUEA Journal* 12. Fall 1984.

Kaplan, H. M. "Farmland: A Non-Traditional Asset?" Mimeographed. AGVEST, undated.

Markowitz, H. M. "Portfolio Selection." *The Journal of Finance* 7. March 1952; pp. 77–91.

————. *Portfolio Selection.* New York: John Wiley & Sons, 1959.

Miller, M. H.; and M. S. Scholes. "Dividends and Taxes." *Journal of Financial Economics* 6. December 1978.

Money Market Directories, Inc., ed., *Real Estate Investing by Pension Funds.* Charlottesville: Money Market Directories, Inc., 1985.

National Council of Real Estate Investment Fiduciaries (NCREIF) and Frank Russell Company. "FRC Property Index." Quarterly.

Sack, P. "Management of Real Estate Portfolios." In *The Investment Manager's Handbook.* Ed. Sumner N. Levine. Homewood: Dow Jones-Irwin, 1980.

Sharpe, W. P. "Bonds vs. Stocks: Some Lessons from Capital Market Theory." *Financial Analysts Journal* 29. November/December 1973.

Thompson, T. "The Property Laws that are Fencing Out Farm-Belt Buyers." *Business Week.* February 18, 1985.

Zerbst, R. H.; and B. R. Cambon. "Real Estate: Historical Returns and Risks." *The Journal of Portfolio Management* 10. Spring 1984.

Seminar proceedings available from Dow Jones-Irwin

**NEW DEVELOPMENTS IN
MORTGAGE-BACKED SECURITIES**
Edited by Frank J. Fabozzi, CFA

☐

The growth of the mortgage-backed securities market has been dramatic in the last five years, and it is continuing to grow. This book explains the investment characteristics, new developments, and strategic use of these instruments. 90 pages, 1985, order no. 2083D.

**OPTIONS AND FUTURES: New Route
to Risk/Return Management**
Edited by Donald E. Fischer, CFA

☐

A comprehensive discussion that covers the nature of futures and options, the participants in the markets, exchange operations, and pricing, as well as strategies for using futures and options in portfolio management. 79 pages, 1984, order no. 1974D.

**IMPROVING THE INVESTMENT DECISION
PROCESS: Quantitative Assistance for
the Practitioner—and for the Firm**
Edited by H. Russell Fogler, Ph.D., and
Darwin M. Bayston, CFA

☐

This is a practical discussion of the effective use of the developing quantitative tools to aid investment decisions. 117 pages, 1984, order no. 1998D.

INTERNATIONAL EQUITY INVESTING
Edited by James R. Vertin, CFA

☐

The diversification opportunities and risk/return potential, as well as the problems and challenges of investing in foreign markets, are explored in this book. 92 pages, 1984, order no. 2014D.

**APPLYING ECONOMIC ANALYSIS
TO PORTFOLIO MANAGEMENT: Improving
the Investment Decision Process**
Edited by James R. Vertin, CFA

☐

The application of economic analysis to portfolio management has long been a challenge to financial analysts. The insights into the role of economics and economists in the investment decision process will prove valuable. 105 pages, 1985, order no. 2104D.

MANAGING THE INVESTMENT PROFESSIONAL
Edited by James R. Vertin, CFA

☐

Managerial methods that provide the environment in which creative investment professionals can work successfully are discussed from the perspective of both the large and small organization. 104 pages, 1984, order no. 2134D.

**THE REVOLUTION IN TECHNIQUES
FOR MANAGING BOND PORTFOLIOS**
Edited by Donald L. Tuttle, CFA

☐

The dynamic strategies for managing bond portfolios since that market's growth and increased volatility in the 1970s are examined in this book. Active and passive management, immunization, bond dedication, and future directions are covered by experienced portfolio managers. 148 pages, 1983, order no. 2153D.

REAL ESTATE INVESTING
Edited by Tom S. Sale III, CFA

☐

Real estate constitutes the largest share of American wealth. *Real Estate Investing* brings together experts with experience in virtually all forms of real estate markets to provide a forum for discussing the unique risk/return characteristics and diversification benefits of this investment option. 102 pages, 1985, order no. 2193D.

The Institute of Chartered Financial Analysts Continuing Education Series

These volumes are sponsored by The Institute of Chartered Financial Analysts and published by Dow Jones-Irwin, an affiliate of Richard D. Irwin, Inc. They are the proceedings of the Institute's Continuing Education seminars held throughout the country in 1983 and 1984. Not only do they make a valuable contribution to the professional literature, but they also provide important material for the CFA candidate study and examination program.

Indicate number of copies wanted in the boxes above.

Total no. of copies ordered _____ @ $25.00 = _____   ☐ Check enclosed

Shipping/handling ($2 first book; $.50 each additional book) _____   ☐ Charge:

Tax (add appropriate tax for CA, IL, NY, TN residents) _____   ☐ Visa

Total enclosed _____   ☐ MasterCard

Mail this form to:
ORDER DEPARTMENT
DOW JONES-IRWIN
1818 RIDGE ROAD
HOMEWOOD, IL 60430

Card no. _____

Exp. date _____

Signature _____

Name _____

Address _____

_____